Notorious Crimes of the Upper Midwest

Notorious Crimes of the Upper Midwest

Con Men, Cutthroats, Killers, and Cannibals

Tom Baker

4880 Lower Valley Road • Atglen, PA 19310

This book is dedicated to the memories of JASON and KIMBERLY TUZINSKI (both 1974–1994), to TRICIA LYNN REITLER (B. 1974. Presumed dead) and to all victims, everywhere. It is likewise dedicated to the slandered and vilified men and women of law enforcement, the "Thin Blue Line" between us and anarchy, who put their lives on the line, day in and day out, to try and hold together the fragmenting pieces of this rapidly declining society.

Background images for pages 5 and 6 have been created by Tom Baker

Library of Congress Control Number: 2017935067

Cover design by Matthew Goodman
Type set in Elephant, Trade Gothic & Minion

ISBN: 978-0-7643-5389-5
Printed in the United States of America

Published by Schiffer Publishing, Ltd.
4880 Lower Valley Road
Atglen, PA 19310
Phone: (610) 593-1777; Fax: (610) 593-2002
E-mail: Info@schifferbooks.com
Web: www.schifferbooks.com

Acknowledgments

Special thanks go to Dinah Roseberry, my longtime editor at Schiffer Books, with warmest regards. Also, my mother, Brenda Durham and my entire family, as well as Sherri Mooney and the staff of the Marion Public Library for their invaluable assistance with research materials. Also, those who have supported my work over the years; warmest regards to you all.

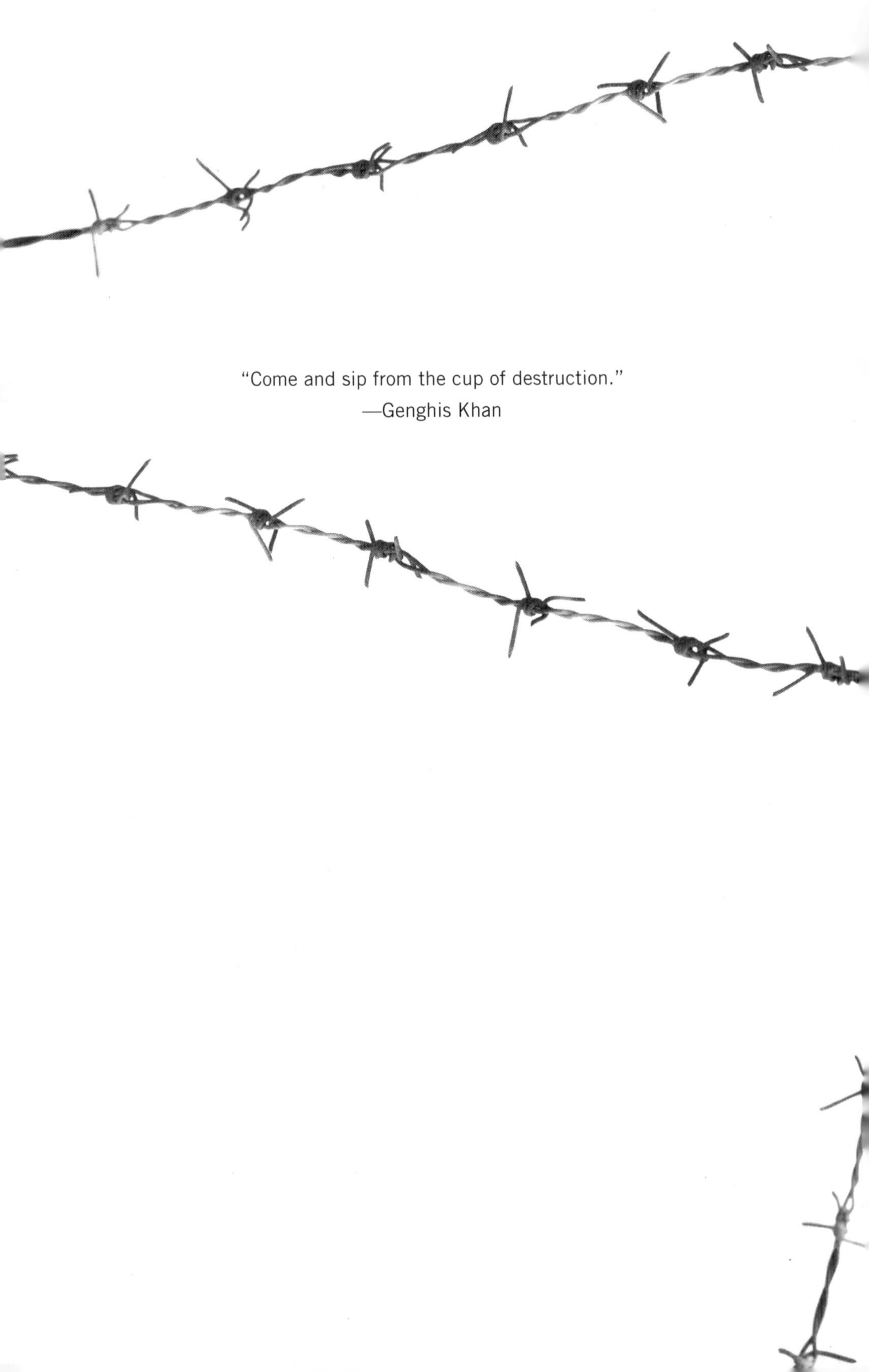

"Come and sip from the cup of destruction."
—Genghis Khan

Contents

PREFACE

Beginnings

Not That There Ever Are Any

For me, I suppose the horror began with a picture of a man whose head had been blown off. It was reprinted in the book *The Edge of Evil* by Maury Terry, which alleged a conspiracy in the Son of Sam murders, one that involved more killers than the lone madman, David Berkowitz.

It was in the late 1980s that I saw that particular grim photo. By the early 1990s, I had seen quite a bit more. Locally, also, young Tricia Lynn Reitler was abducted while walking across the campus of Indiana Weslyan University in my hometown of Marion, Indiana, on March 29, 1993. A year later, a man named Larry Dewayne Hall, imprisoned for a similar crime, would confess repeatedly to killing her. Hall is a large, ungainly fellow serving life without parole in federal prison. He is suspected of dozens of abductions and sex killings.

The story of Larry Hall is detailed in the book *Urges* by Christopher Hawley Martin. While I was reading that book, perhaps reminiscing about those bygone days of the '90s, I had a dream one night wherein I was a teacher at a school for disabled children. I have been a teacher in the past, so it sort of makes sense. I was tasked with cleaning out a filthy cage in back of the place, a rabbit coop or hutch or whatever they call them. It was old and rusted, and sinking into the mud. And so I got filthy trying to clean out this festering cage of dying, half-starved rabbits ("Wabbits"), and another teacher comes up and asks how I am doing. I say okay, but ask what they do with the bodies of these dead rabbits. I am told: "They haul them away, I think. Turn them into meat glue."

Surprised and disgusted, I asked, "And they are actually eaten?"

To which she replied, "Everything in nature is eaten, eventually."

Yes.

Introductory Note

This book serves no specific ideological viewpoint, nor does it attempt to be a definitive or chronological history of crime. It focuses on a particular geographical location, but it does not limit its scope to that area alone. Lastly, it does not present the subject matter in any particular specific historical perspective—these articles were written almost as a collection of individual magazine articles, not to build, one on the other, era after era.

Thus, you'll find we skip back and forth in time quite a bit here. *C'est la vie!*

CHAPTER 1

An Epoch of Homicide

This is my third book on the subject of multiple murderers.

I'm not sure why this subject keeps calling me home. If anything, I find it rather depressing, rather numbing in an intellectual sense. There is really nothing to be learned, by and large, from rubbernecking at the site of a grisly accident. A tale of murder is no different. No matter the underlying motive for the crime, it still remains a brutal, senseless, stupid act, a curiosity to be examined in the light of the actions performed by those with better hearts and minds.

In other words, those who can intellectually contrast it with the niceties of civilization: the clean, calm, cool, and sterile humanistic world of color television, fast-food shops, green lawns, happy subdivisions, and retail stores full of consumer products and technological wizardry. (We've come a long way, baby.)

In the dark, somewhere, even as you read these words, someone is burying a body. He (most likely it is a he) is breaking the ground with the cold, rusted tip of a spade, is shoveling out buckets of earth. He has given into the compulsion yet again, has gone on auto-pilot as the hideous "thing" inside of himself has taken control, has reared its ugly head like a dragon, has lashed out at the world again, has taken a "victim." It could be a prostitute, or a luckless hitchhiker, a street kid, perhaps. Whatever the case, they have been sacrificed on the altar of this individual's psychopathy. They are the result of many years of pent-up torments, isolated voices, abuse, terror, hatred, and a growing inferno of rage that, vampie-like, is only sated by the thirst for living blood.

Society may be at fault, or even God. Believers in ultimate evil will undoubtedly wonder at the reality of demonic possession, of the fabled Father of Lies and his nefarious doings; others will blame capitalism, Marxism, liberalism, divorce, television, heavy metal bands, Dungeons and Dragons, etc.

Some will say that it is simply the *Nature of the Beast*. By "Beast," we mean "Man" (in the non-gender exclusive sense).

Some will question whether the author, who, admittedly is no criminologist, is really fully qualified to write endlessly about this subject. The author would offer a rejoinder that he is, in point of fact, eminently qualified for such an undertaking as, although he has never personally murdered anyone and never will, he is, nonetheless, quite familiar with the sort of monstrous alienation that can, in many cases, lead an errant or undisciplined spirit onto the path of perdition—of great and monstrous sin. (And your author is very much a believer in sin; oh yes indeed.)

I am an introvert, a recluse; I don't really make friends. I have no children, no romantic relationships, and haven't had any for a very long time. Furthermore, if I could move to an island and find a more complete solitude (and hope to survive) I would, by all means, do so. To say much more would turn this introduction into a biography, and that wouldn't do. Suffice it to say, though I am nominally a Christian, I have trouble embracing humanistic values. (Christian ethics often seem the ideological twin of Marxism, and I detest Marxism.)

I am a social misfit—a loner. So, in a strange sense, though I am certainly no criminal, I understand, full well, what drives the lonely, the isolated, the ostracized . . . the fringe dwellers and the social outcasts. I've been there.

We live in an epoch of homicide. A\ spate of school and workplace shootings, including a bizarre and horrific mass murder at a Connecticut elementary school, have plagued our society in recent years. Serial killers seem old hat; a Jack the Ripper seems corny and trite compared to Adam Lanza, a weird, skeletal punk who took out *five* times as many victims in a few hours as Jack seemingly did in his entire career. Overseas, militant

Islamic radicals have taken to crucifying and beheading people, burning them alive on video, mowing down civilization in a path of destruction that seems more the actions of medieval barbarians than modern men.

Reports indicate the current dictator of North Korea had his uncle fed to wild dogs. (And the man does love to flaunt his nuclear capabilitiea and missile technology.)

Domestically, cops are in the doghouse due to a string of questionable killings. Riots and looting have plagued major cities, an eccentric real estate tycoon may be the latest tired installment of "capture a serial killer," and the news still occasionally sparkles with sightings of the woman who was acquitted a few years ago for murdering her toddler (although everyone with half a functioning brain realizes she was . . . well, you know). Truly, we live in an era of murder.

Terrorism.

School shootings.

Wars and rumors of wars . . .

I present to you twenty profiles in ignominy, selections from the lives of the serial killers, as well as an assassin and hired gun or two. To maintain regional appeal I have selected criminals primarily from the Midwestern region, with a special concentration on the Upper Midwestern states. If I occasionally stray from this during the course of this tome, please forgive me; murder and vice know no set geographical locations, as I'm sure you are already aware.

What I *will* do is entertain you, I hope. In much the same way as the Ancient Roman was glutted to the full capabilities of his sensory organs on the sounds and spectacles of the Circus Maximus, so too must I be glutted on the dark doings and depraved happenings of our dissolute and damaged history. I am simply fulfilling a role, carrying on a tradition began, long, long ago, in the blood-spattered, thunderous pages of penny dreadfuls authored by men like Frank Tripplett, who begot the legend of Jesse James.

I will inform, but I will also *Feed the Beast*. I walk an ethical tightrope; if, that is, art has anything to do with ethics. (Black magician Aliester Crowley once famously observed, in a court of law no less, that art and morality had *nothing* whatsoever to do with each other. Ironically, the disposition of his libel suit was that Crowley was declared "libel-proof"; in other words, his lifestyle was so bizarre, notorious, and outre, nothing anyone said about him could possibly make his reputation any worse! Or, so was the decision of the presiding magistrate.)

Hence, I am, almost as always, in the business of *selling horrors*. Or, maybe put it another way, peddling fear to an anxiety-ridden public. They wanted it when they lined up for movies like Frankenstein in the 1940s; they want it still.

After all, what else would you expect in an epoch of homicide?

—Tom Baker,
May 26, 2015

CHAPTER 2

The Nauseating Nurses

Gwendolyn Graham and Kathy Wood

M Is for Mary

The old lady struggled a little, her withered, corpse-like hands climbing to the pillow, trying in desperation to pull the thing from her face.

Gwen held firm, her grip steady and true. This was exciting. This was retribution. This was going to mark them out, make them somebodies. At least, that was the fantasy. It was all one, with a fantasy of lounging around a swimming pool, sipping champagne with Martha. Two young chickas, in tight bikini bathing suits, basking anonymously in the Florida sunshine. Cool, placid water reflecting their images, their beautiful images, forever taut and tanned bodies oiled and sleeked-down with suntan lotion, and cared-for and primed.

Alternately, they had a fantasy of being surrounded on all sides by the cops. Two doomed lovers: Bonnie and Clyde-deal. Or, more appropriately, Bonnie and Bonnie.

Going out in a blaze of glory, hail of bullets.

The old bitch struggled feebly, shuddered. Gave up the ghost, she did. M is for Mary.

U Is for Ursulla

They had met at Alpine Valley. She had been taken, almost immediately by her looks, her striking, penetrating gaze, the tough, no-nonsense exterior. She had been lonely. She was a lesbian, a dyke, and, in 1986, that was still something you didn't readily advertise.

So, she warmed up to Gwen pretty quickly. It started off as little love notes, mash notes. Real hot stuff. Then, the poem: "I'll love you, forever and a day."

Then it was sex.

More . . .

"You ever thought about the things that connect people? Those things that they do together, that they can never undo?"

She had no idea what the hell Gwen was talking about. Outside, somebody down the street was shouting drunkenly as an engine revved.

"Like, a thing . . . something people can do together, to bond them together. Like . . . like a secret they can never share.

I'll love you . . . forever and a day.

Kathy rolled over, looked at her lover, asked, innocently enough, "Just what did you have in mind?"

R Is for Roberta

(I had a grandmother who died of Alzheimer's Disease. In her final stages, she was incapacitated on a couch, moving her limbs involuntarily, completely unconscionable to the world. Before this, she would do things such as fix food that was improperly prepared [she would, for instance, forget and leave massive, grotesque chicken bones in a pot of noodles], and also fail to recognize her own family members. It goes without saying that such people are easy targets.)

She sits there with an empty, vacant look in the eye. Her family might come to see her. Maybe not. Either way, she'd never be able to recognize them anyway. Gwendolyn feeds her, ramming an immense spoon of puree down her throat, not delicately. The stuff slobbers all over her chin. A fly dots to and fro across her pale, wrinkled, spotted visage. The dull, vacant eyes stare listlessly as the nurse ladles out sustaining nourishment. The toothless maw sucks the gravy down. Gwendolyn might retch.

"I have to wipe their asses, change their diapers, feed them their slop. I take them for their whirlpool baths, make sure they don't get bedsores.

"Once, one of them died on my watch. Cancer, I think. Old bitch must have started rotting from the inside out some time before. I mean, I've never smelled a smell like that. It permeated everything, wafted up and down the hallways. Nursing home staff is used to this shit, but I saw people gagging, running to the bathroom to puke . . ."

She looked at her own image in the cracked mirror over the washbasin. Mouth too big, eyes too wide. Manly woman. Lesbian. *Dyke.*

Behind her, Cathy said, "Who are you talking to, Gwendolyn?"

She didn't really know.

"I have a permanent monologue going on, up here. It's a sign, you know."

Cathy approached, said, "A sign. A sign of what?"

"Insanity," Gwen answered flatly.

Cathy grasped her shoulders, pulled her close.

"I'll love you . . . forever and a day."

R is for Roberta, who barely moved a muscle when they stuffed the rag over her mouth and nose.

D Is for Dying

Cathy noted: "It was too difficult to keep killing them based on the first letters of their names. So we decided to do them based on the days of the week. I acted as the lookout, and Gwen was the one that did the actual . . . It was usually holding a pillow or rag over their head. Those people, they couldn't fight. Most of them were close to being vegetables anyway. Gwen thought we were doing the world a favor. And maybe we were doing them a favor, too. I mean, would you want to live if you were just a vegetable that couldn't take care of yourself? How degrading. This way, we felt we were giving them some sort of dignity."

They got hot for each other, bathing down those corpses. It was a real kick, they decided, cleaning up your little mess, and knowing, deep inside, as you shared the deep, stagnant water fluid of your partner, that you had, for just a minute, a little bit of your own against a world that wouldn't accept you. A world that never cared.

The bodies were old, withered; they didn't smell like roses. Cleaning the shit and filth from them was a grotesque job, one that would require a strong stomach, an even stronger nerve.

The faces were frozen in the rictus of agony in which they had departed, their presumable souls stealing down the vacant, piss-stinking hallways of Alpine, to a presumable "light." Or, perhaps darkness. Or perhaps they wandered the hallways, confused, lost—alone.

"They died in confusion," Gwen might have pondered aloud. "Do you think their souls even realize they've gone?"

Somehow, the closeness, the intimacy of cleaning the bodies of the departed, gave them an extra fillip of macabre satisfaction, made their lovemaking—

"Something spiritual. Something just a little bit . . . beyond."

Cathy (who was obese and under the heavy psychological domination of her lover) simply quoted her poem: "I'll love you forever and a day. Forever is a long, long time, baby."

The two kissed in a room that stank of corpses.

D is for Dying.

They had that one shored up at both ends.

E Is for Evil

(I herein relate a fictional montage of several key factors hitherto not considered, but now deemed essential to painting a more complete, if sordid, portrait.)

Cathy was fat. It was taking every bit of her strength to diet the pounds away. But Gwen didn't seem to mind—"As long as you keep trying. That's what's important in life. That, and having a good attitude."

Cathy arched a curious eyebrow.

"Is that why you always tell those sick jokes? Telling on us? Confessing?"

Gwen considered.

"I . . . I do that because I find it heightens the intensity of the game. I mean, this is a game we're playing, right? A sex game? Like when I tie you up and tie the knot around your neck. It makes the arousal so much more intense, the orgasm so much sweeter."

Cathy said, "Mhm. More of an edge."

In the living room of the dump they shared, a single shelf of dentures and bracelets and other trophies from their victims was displayed proudly, for visitors.

†

"Hey Reggie."

Gwen was addressing Reggie, a male nurse. She quite suspected he was a swish.

"Huh?"

"I ever tell you about the old bitch I suffocated. Sure. Stuck a rag down her throat. Watched her squirm. These Alzheimer's patients, man, they're just like little children: they can't fight back. It's their weakness that makes it, oh, so sweet."

Reggie looked at her with a bleary, bloodshot eye. He was mercilessly hung over, and this bitch wasn't helping. Her and her sick jokes.

"Uh, okay, Gwen baby. Whatever you say."

"Yep," she agreed cheerily. "Whatever I say. Better not cross me Reggie, or I'll fucking kill you."

(Gwen had been molested by her father as a youngster. This led, some might hypothesize, to her ritualistic masochism, which involved cutting and burning herself with cigarettes. Such behavior is not uncommon, it has been pointed out, among "borderline" personality types. The author is well aware of this, remembering his own youthful days in an institution, exposed to two "cutters."

One, a thickset, Hispanic girl with grotesquely scarred arms, sat across a table from a tall, lanky, blonde metal head type in an '80s [it was 1989] rock band tee. The boy had smuggled in a metal necklace as well as a razor blade.

> Before my rather naive gaze, they cut fairly superficial gashes in their skin, leaving trickling smears of blood. At one point, the Hispanic girl [who sported a for-the-time wild punk cut that looked as if she'd caught the sides of her head in a blender] implored the metal head to "Break out Mr. Gillette" [his smuggled-in razor blade].
>
> (The two cretins took turns carving themselves with superficial cuts. This was in the day room, right under the nose of the clueless night shift staff.)

Now: "The Shotgun/Vagina Episode"

No one is quite certain who put the shotgun to whose vagina. Although we assume it was Gwen (who, in a documentary this author has seen, a couple of researchers/crime writers go out of their way to exonerate, laying the blame for all the murderous mischief on the porcine shoulders of the luckless Cathy—currently still serving her twenty-year sentence).

All we can say with any degree of certainty is that *someone* put a *shotgun* up someone's vagina. Cathy points the finger at Gwen, who likewise points the finger at Cathy. What could possibly have precipitated the alleged shotgun/vagina episode is hard to say. Was it merely another sick thrill to heighten the intensity of sexual arousal? Was it a threat, a warning to stay faithful, a way for Gwen (alternately Cathy) to exercise more control? This author must rely solely on conjecture, with the added stipulation that, whoever shoved said shotgun into the other's bodily orifice, it certainly is just one small example of a long list of indicators that the women were in a markedly pathological relationship.

It would be tiresome to trifle with exactly *why* Cathy left Gwen. Gwen was, apparently, showing interest in another woman. Gwen moved to Texas, at any rate. Cathy kept in contact with her former lover, although she also began to resume relations with an ex-husband.

It was the ex who was instrumental in getting Cathy to confess. Another prompt was: "I wonder what it would be like to *smash an infant against a wall*?"

Gwen supposedly said this. She had begun working as a caregiver at a children's home.

(One indeed gets the mental image from *Andy Warhol's Bad*, in which there is a scene depicting an infant tossed from the window of a high rise apartment. The special effect was not so special—a burst watermelon. But such a drop, indeed, would be a horrifying, sickening mess in real life.)

We're still captivated, ourselves, by the mental image of the shotgun in the vagina. Like a cheap, sleazy scene from a porno film, the sort smuggled in from South America, the scene unfolds . . .

Gwen stands, rigid, "Take it bitch! Take it all up your fucking cunt! You like that, huh bitch? You ever leave me, or betray me, you'll get this right where it is now, And then *I'll pull the trigger*."

(The same woman, supposedly, who asked what smashing an infant against a wall would "be like.")

The legs are splayed at right angles. Maybe the posture is rigid, the lips are curled back and the eyes half-lidded in the pleasure of the cold steel. Of being used, dominated; abused and threatened in a way that made life and death one sensual whole.

She might have been terrified. Or, she might have moaned, like some bored actress in a porn flick, that she wanted it deeper and harder.

We don't know.

Cathy's ex-husband went directly to the police. They went directly to Gwen, who was arrested in her hometown of Tyler, Texas. Cathy was likewise arrested, and the arrest (har-har) is history.

Gwen pointed the finger at Cathy.

Cathy pointed the finger at Gwen.

Crime writers and experts seem to agree that Cathy Wood is one manipulative bitch.

Que sera, sera.

Gwen is doing life in Michigan. Cathy is still seeking parole. Possibly is overdue for it.

R Is for Retribution

Given what society has devolved into, the term "social misfit" has lost a lot of its sting since I was a little kid.

However, in 1986, to be a social outcast, for any reason, was still something that carried with it a certain feeling of shame, opprobrium—a certain stigma. Not to the degree it did in say, 1956, but the feeling of social shaming was still there.

It seemed that Gwen and Cathy, as lesbians, were going to feel the brunt of that social stigma keenly. How much animosity does it take before someone goes over the edge? Snaps? Feels they are so far outside the regular social milieu that any action, no matter how grievous, heinous, or antisocial, is a justifiable slap back at a society that, fundamentally, has no place for them?

You could argue up one blood-spattered wall and down the other. In the case of Gwen and Cathy, however, the "law always wins," (to quote that great American purveyor of belles-lettres, Ms. Bonnie Parker), as both women were sent for long, long (in the case of Gwen, permanent) prison sentences.

Gwen was convicted and sent up for five consecutive life sentences to a women's facility in Michigan.

Cathy, who rolled over on her ex-lover, was still slapped with a couple of decades in a (curiously) federal prison in Florida. According to online resources, she is overdue for parole.

One blames the other, and vice-versa.

Crime writers seem to exonerate Gwen based on a rather weak, easily-manipulated mentality. Or, supposedly this is one of her true characteristics.

This writer doesn't know either way.

He just loves pouring through sordid laundry (the type you might find in, oh, I dunno, a nursing home) looking for bugs.

CHAPTER 3

Homicidal Heartbreak

Raymond Fernandez and Martha Beck

Few people today probably remember a sleazy, black-and- white cult film from 1969 called The Honeymoon Killers. This author saw it in 1997, on VHS, rented from the Dave's Video across the street from what is now the CVS Pharmacy, in lovely downtown Marion, Indiana. Dave's Video, and its videotape assortment of oddball Mexican horror films, "shockumentaries," and general sordid and forgotten gems is long gone, a victim of YouTube and the encroaching Internet age. But, for a short time, it reigned supreme in our search for cheap thrills.

Martha Beck (portrayed in the film by forgotten actress Shirley Stoler) works in a psychiatric hospital for wayward youth. Obese and ungainly, she combs the "Lonely Hearts" section of the newspapers, looking for love "in all the wrong places." Unfortunately for her, she finds it in the form of Raymond Fernandez, a balding, disreputable man described by police detectives as a " seedy Charles Boyer" type, down on his luck.

Fernandez had, remarkably, once worked for military intelligence. That is, until a head injury during the war caused an erratic change in mood and personality. Granted a discharge, he elected not to return to his native Hawaii but instead embarked for Michigan for obscure reasons.

It was here he began to ply the sordid trade for which history (criminal history, that is) would forever remember him. Becoming a confidence trickster (what we would today term a "con man"), he put ads in the "Lonely Hearts" sections of various newspapers hoping to hook a fish. He found himself the bitter, lonely whale of a woman named Martha. And this set the stage for his murderous misadventure.

†

Raymond and Martha disported to Michigan, trailing a promising victim. Raymond would woo them, the "seedy Charles Boyer" laying on the Latin charm thick and heavy, and Martha, poor, jealous Martha, would skulk in the background, confined to the role of a "sister," bitter and suspicious of the motives of her crooked paramour.

In time, Raymond Fernandez would convince these lonely, elderly women that they should marry him. Signing over their life savings to the felonious gigolo, he and Martha would then beat a hasty retreat, richer it would seem, but none the wiser. When and where they crossed over into murder is anyone's guess. But so they did.

It was in Grand Rapids, Michigan, in 1949, where what was done in the dark was suddenly, brightly illuminated by the severe searchlight of the lawful authorities. But, perhaps, we can set the stage for our little drama by stating boldly that Martha was even more insanely jealous than usual, Raymond in this case wooing a young (twenty-eight), somewhat attractive woman named Delphine Dowling. Delphine had a two-year-old daughter, and this must have complicated matters, too.

"We should wait to get married," Delphine croons (or so we imagine!) "I want to know if your love is true. If it is everything you say it is!"

And Raymond might answer, bent over the couch, or on one knee, his black wig cocked across his cold, clammy brow, "But darling, I do love you! More than you could ever know! More than all the great lovers of the past have loved, I love you! You are my Desdemona, my Juliet, my angel . . ."

Blah, blah, blah. (I'm not, myself, familiar with the language of romantic wooing . . . does anyone still speak it in this coarse, vulgar day and age? I don't know. But I guess the slimy charm of Raymond Fernandez would possibly conjure a scene like the one depicted here.)

Later, in their private room, when Delphine had been "dosed" to sleep by the massive, morose Martha, Raymond and his "sister" would discuss such things as: "Don't you dare wait. She has to go! Now! She could cause us a lot of trouble! Matter of fact, I think she's starting to get suspicious. What if she changes her mind, throws us out? Then we've wasted all this time, and we'll have nothing to show for the effort."

Raymond, taking off his shoes, would say, "Yes, yes! I agree. But, we must be careful! Let's wait a little longer, plan accordingly . . . I mean, where are we to dispose of the body, for instance?"

They found a place. They concocted a simple plan.

Martha tucked Delphine in real nice one night. Maybe she offered her a customary cup of cocoa, maybe some wine. At any rate, she had crushed enough sleeping pills into the concoction to ensure her beauty rest would be eternal.

That was that!

†

"My momma! Where's my momma? I want my momma!"

The two-year-old was inconsolable. Martha wanted to crush her head under one of her porky, pig-like little hands. She knew how to deal with brats; after all she had run a home for crippled children at one point, hadn't she?

"No," protested Raymond. "It's no good. Here, let's try to please her somehow, make her like us. I know! Let's buy her a puppy! All children love puppies!"

And so . . .

(History does not record what became of the puppy. I can only hope a good home was found for it later by authorities. But, maybe Martha and Raymond took it outside and bashed its brains out with a hammer. Really, though, does this last seem in character, or no?)

"Where's my momma? I want my momma!"

The child continued to fuss and cause problems. Raymond and Martha, not so sure keeping the brat alive was such a good idea (after all, she was tying them down, and they really needed to be away, to be gone), suddenly decided that the baby's two-year-old life was now to be snuffed short.

"A bath. You need a bath. Ugh, you smell terrible! Your momma told me to give you a bath. She said she wanted you to be clean and tidy for when she returned.

The trusting child soon dried her tears, and, lifting up her arms, allowed Martha Beck to strip her bare. Martha ran the water in the tub, all the while cooing, "There, there, you're gonna be all cleaned up and smell so good for when your momma comes home! And won't she be happy when she sees you? Why, I bet she'll give you a big hug, huh? Now, I want you to dip your toe in here, so's to make sure it ain't too hot."

The child did as instructed, finally sliding into the water. Any thinking person would have to wonder if there was a moment, a bare moment, when a flicker of conscience stalled her heavy, porky fingers. Was there a moment, perched upon the precipice of this most terrible act of infanticide, when even a monstrous being like Martha stalled, retreated, refused, for a bare moment, to slide any deeper down the path toward perdition?

A cynical person, a person familiar with the curious nature of human evil, will already know the answer.

The child thrashed and fought as Martha held her under the water; but a child has no chance of escaping the clutches of someone who has decided to end its life, so it was most decidedly the child's time to go.

Martha must have dried off her meaty forearms, and then went to Raymond to decide where the bodies should be buried.

They finally decided to bury mother and daughter in the cellar. Their mistake was not then fleeing as quickly and quietly as they could; instead, they lingered like malicious phantoms for days, and finally faced the probing questions of police; who, immediately alerted by the strange, sullen couple, returned with a search warrant, post-haste.

They examined the cellar. They found the shallow graves. Martha and her murderous paramour freely confessed everything.

What Do the Public Know of Love?

A sweaty, candid interview with Raymond Fernandez followed. He copped to one murder after another, feeling exuberant, perhaps, to finally get it all off of his chest. In this way, he is much like Judd Grey, the lonely, embittered and penitent accomplice of New York murderess Ruth Snyder, who conspired in 1928 to murder her husband in what hardboiled mystery writer James M. Cain later used as the basis for his famous novel Double Indemnity (later a movie with Fred MacMurry, Edward G. Robinson, and Barbara Stanwyck). Jay Robert Nash amusingly notes that Raymond was sweating so profusely at one point that he took off his wig, using it to mop his dripping brow.

Martha was equally loquacious, but complained that she received only a few grand from their last killing. (One wonders where she thought they would spend their blood money at this point, anyway.)

Neither of them seemed overly concerned with the prospect of life in prison—and they were certain that, as Michigan did *not* have the death penalty, that was all they would get for their trail of innumerable bodies. Little did they know, or at least, take into account, the fact that New York *did* have the death penalty, and that Michigan was more than happy to allow the both of them to be extradited to stand trial for a murder committed there.

Extradited they were. Both were jointly condemned to die at Sing-Sing in the electric chair.

Ironically, when asked if he still loved Martha, Raymond replied indignantly that, of course he did, adding, somewhat poetically, "I wanna shout it out; I love Martha! What do the public know about love?"

What indeed.

We can think of few couples who went to the gallows (in this case, the electric chair) virtually together. Julius and Ethel Rosenberg, the Cold War-era spies convicted of passing nuclear secrets to the Soviets; and of course Snyder and Grey. Grey went a repentant wretch to his death, bolstering his flagging courage with religious ejaculations and professions of redemption, faith, and eternal life. Ruth Snyder, a Catholic, apparently made confession or took communion first. Cameras were to be banned in the death chamber when these two were killed, minutes apart from each other.

An enterprising reporter, however, managed to rig an ingenious device: a "shoe camera" that could be clicked from a string up his leg. Miraculously, this device was not detected by law enforcement officers upon the man's entry as a witness to the execution.

The resultant photograph, taken the moment the switch was thrown on Ruth Snyder, is horrific to those who discover it for the first time: a thickset female form, wearing what appears to be a hideous rubber face mask (to keep the eyes from popping out with the electrical discharge, perhaps?) strapped down into the chair, her soul ejected from her body on a white hot thunderclap of killing electrical force. The photo appeared on the front page of a tabloid rag, becoming an overnight sensational shocker. It is the first photograph ever taken of someone in the electric chair, at the moment of death.

But, back to Raymond and Martha.

Raymond spent the last night of his life refusing food, worried that he would vomit everything back up in fear and despair. He smoked an enormous Havana cigar down to a stub, and then nearly collapsed. He was half-carried to the death chamber, unable to stand up under the weight of a fate he had sealed by his own evil actions.

Martha, for her part, was more resilient, more determined to give off a paean of control, put on an air of cold indifference in the face of her own death. She, at first, likewise refused a meal. Then, apparently, she thought, "What the hell!" and ordered a double portion of fried chicken and mashed potatoes, finishing her final, grim repast, and going with stoic resolution to the chair. Author Jay Robert Nash gives us a portrait of Martha's considerable bulk as she sat it down in Ol' Sparky, treating us to a comic-grotesque image of how it "heaved and groaned" under her weight. Whether it did or not we do not know (this could be, as in the case of Albert Fish and the supposed "blue sparks" that shot forth from the chair when he was executed—supposed to have been due to the needles the demented old wretch had shoved into his scrotum—nothing but mere criminal folklore); nor do we think it matters a great deal. The smiling, defiant Martha was rendered just as dead, a few moments later.

The date? March 8, 1951.

Martha, for her part, confessed undying love for Raymond. Perhaps they both found each other in the afterlife, pushing onward into whatever eternal dungeon or cycle of karmic rebirth had in store for the two murderous sweethearts. Such may be the power of true love. Not that any of us, Dear Reader, could really understand.

After all, what do the public know about love?

CHAPTER 4

The Hardcase

The Despicable Life and Deserved Death of Carl Panzram

There is no way to properly quantify a Carl Panzram. More a demonic force of nature than a living man, Panzram embodied all that is most hateful, bitter, malignant, and vile in the human spirit.

His motto was "rob 'em all, rape 'em all, and kill 'em all." And he meant every damn syllable of it. His hands had gripped many a throat, his fists had bashed out many brainpans, and his devious, psychotic brain had envisioned murders on an atrocious scale. (One of his fantasies was derailing a train, and, as the surviving passengers poured out of the wrecked choo-choo, of gunning them all down in an orgy of bloodletting. Or, maybe he wanted to use a flame thrower. I can't now exactly remember.)

Carl is not legendary in the same way some of the famous serial killers of the past have become; he is no Jack the Ripper, for instance. Almost no one walking the street would recognize his name if you spoke it to them. Yet, his has been referred to as a "Gorgonian odyssey of crime," and his story has been celebrated in art by underground PAINter Joe Coleman, as well as in film. His character was played by venerated actor James Woods in the small film Killer: A Journal of Murder, which was executive produced by Oliver Stone.

To begin his story, we must say he was raised on a farm in Minnesota, with a worthless father who soon abandoned the family. He went to school drunk at age eight. From there, it was all a rather downward spiral for young Carl Panzram, a person who would grow to tower as a veritable ogre of monstrous sadism and hate.

He learned while in reform school that the system was cruel and hard to those who stood against it. He burned down a wood shed, one oft used for "disciplining" boys in the harshest, cruelest way. No, no one ever found out that it was he, little troublemaker Carl, that had done that particular act. Nor did they suspect that he would graduate to greater, much more deadly enterprises.

†

Carl eventually fled his Minnesota home. What the hell, he tired of the strict discipline, the unending toil, the presence of his brother (who would, himself, become a law officer). He took to the rails, the deadly real-life embodiment of the character "Jack Black," as portrayed in another true-crime classic, You Can't Win, about the life of an itinerant thief and hobo, a "bindlestiff." Carl rode the rails; he, according to his later confessions, was raped by drunken hobos.

> (This last must have forged even harder, more maniacal links in the chain of his armor. It would, of course, not be the last such incident in the life of Carl Panzram; in time, though, he would write boastingly that he had himself gone on from this incident to rape nearly a thousand men and boys.)

A play-by-play of Carl's arrests and criminal odyssey would be tedious and tiresome. His life established a pattern of wandering and imprisonment for short stretches. It was in these brutal, turn-of-the-century confines that Carl soon developed the bottomless hatred of humanity that would carry him forth, make him an indomitable ogre of barbarity, a killing machine on two feet whose animalistic rage would be summed up by him, in a succinct fashion as "the spirit of meanness." Indeed he was.

It was during these stretches in jail that Carl was exposed to brutal punishments such as the hot box, floggings, restraints, and the "straight jacket," a tight fitting garment wrapped around the inmate, who, in short order, felt as if he were being suffocated. Some even compared it, in their insanity, to the sensation of being buried alive.

> (Interestingly, a man named Ed Morell became famous for having this done to him while a prisoner, mainly due to his alleged "out-of-body" or even near-death experience during the episode. Morell claimed to have left his body while in the straight jacket, to have traveled outside of prison walls, and to have seen things and met people he could later confirm as really existing. Upon being released from prison, Ed wrote about his experience.)

It was experiences and treatment such as this that confirmed Panzram, a man already twisted at the root from his hideous, unhappy childhood, as the wretched fiend he would become.

†

Petty crimes and short, brutal periods of incarceration were the norm in his life; and, with each step down the pathway toward perdition, toward that final, unyielding, bottomless hatred of mankind, Carl Panzram deliberated the destruction of the reviled humanity he so despised.

"My only wish is that you all had one neck, and that I could get my hands around it," he would later write in his own confessions. And Carl was just being candid.

Carl joined the military for a short period, but was inevitably ousted for drunkenness. Worse, he was imprisoned for a continual pattern of insubordination, sentenced to eighteen long months in Leavenworth Federal Pen, where, he claims, "all the humanity was burned out of me." (That might be a bit of a paraphrase, but I can't find the exact quote just at the moment. At any rate, you get the idea.)

†

I don't know what the day was like when Carl Panzram went to meet the putative maker of the humanity he so despised. It might have been, like the scene in the movie Intolerance, filmed thirteen or fourteen years earlier, a gallows built in a prison room—or, more melodramatically, it might have echoed the tiny details of a classic, fictional hanging, with crows circling overhead, suspended in a bleak, barren sky, as the condemned man is led, with a hood on his head, to the rope, which is quickly placed over his doomed soon-to-be-broken neck.

If a Lillian Gish and her cohorts were racing a locomotive, such as in Intolerance, in order to swoop down with a governor's pardon and prevent the man from being executed at the literal last minute, I've never heard of it. At least not in Carl's case. Indeed, everyone on Earth was pretty happy to see him off—including Carl Panzram himself.

"Hurry it up, you Hoosier bastard! I could kill twenty men while you're messing around with that rope!"

These were, reportedly, Carl's last words.

I seem to only be able to write about Carl Panzram in a fashion that places the essentials of him feet first. Or, maybe put another way, in bite-sized morsels of truth. A timeline review is a bit much for us, in his case.

Carl, by the Roaring Twenties, was already a confirmed killer and sodomizer of men and boys (possibly women too, but what I know primarily from his infamy is his predilection for destroying other males. Certainly there must be something Freudian here.)

Carl confessed, for instance, to the casual murder of a boy who was "bumming around . . . looking for something." What this something was, we are never told, but Carl, seizing his opportunity, or perhaps just acting on the ravening impulse of his distorted soul, raped the boy repeatedly, then bashed his brains out. "When I left him, his brains were leaking out of his ears, and he will *never be any deader*." (Emphasis mine.)

And this is only one incident of countless others. Carl Panzram's life, truly, was soaked in blood.

The ogre, who seems, even to readers and historians today, almost simultaneously superhuman and subhuman, might very well indeed have had "all the goodness burned out of him"; his torture at the hands of those who imprisoned him must have sent him into a hot, bright-white inner core of hatred, a place inside of himself where nothing, no hurt could ever touch him, because no human feeling could ever touch him. For example:

One torture Carl describes in his itinerant tour of the various penalogical institutions of our fine country (circa 1900–1928, or so) was the "Hummingbird," a device in which the unfortunate inmate was immersed in a tub of ice water, while the electrodes from a nearby battery were applied to the skin. After hours of this excruciating torture, the victim was, typically, ready for the grave or the madhouse, to paraphrase Carl.

(Note: As I complete this chapter, the country is in the throes of a panic brought about by the December 2nd massacre of fourteen people at a facility for the disabled. This act was perpetrated, so the story now goes, by Middle Eastern terrorists—albeit ones that were in this country legally, who had acquired their weapons legally. It seems that every time I sit down to work on this book, another tragedy hits the news concurrently, yet another example of the "epoch of homicide." But, this is a digression.)

Carl spent time in South America as a laborer. That he continued his criminal spree here seems to go without saying; he was another roughneck working the oil fields. In such places he most likely had his pick of easy prey, the memory of the white hot electrified sponge of the "hummingbird," or the wounds that were salted at Leavenworth, or any other number of cruel, bizarre, and inhumane practices still echoing in the white-hot spaces behind his thick, demented skull.

†

To give an example, because one is needed, surely: Carl commandeered a yacht, or chartered it (or however the hell you want to put it) and put in with a number of sailors on the East Coast. Going out, getting them roaring drunk, he commenced to rob and sodomize them, or at least as many as he could, (how he managed this amid such a profusion of able-bodied men, is Carl's own private mystery) and then absconded with their loot. And this was only one stop on the Panzram Rock n' Roll World Tour of his exploration of the outer fringes of crime.

Quite similarly, as a merchant seaman off the coast of an African country, he scouted an expedition into the far reaches of the jungle taking along a number of local guides. (To look for buried treasure? One wonders just what the hell he told the natives to get them to accompany him.)

While trudging through the thick, hot foliage of the jungle, swatting at flies, bathing in whiskey, and smelling to high heaven, the deep, psychopathic urge to inflict pain, to erase the human lives of those who had abused him (he must have seen *all* faces as *one* face) overcame his reason.

Whether he had planned it or not, Carl produced his pistol, killed and sodomized (in that order?) his guides, and tossed their innocent bodies into the murk of a river, to be feasted on by the crocodiles.

. . . Leaving the reader to wonder: Can any of this be believed?

If the confessions had come from anyone except the yawning void that was Carl Panzram, this author would be tempted to say . . . no. But, take a look at the face, the eyes; while every picture of Panzram is, undoubtedly, a mug shot, there is a genuine complete lack of moral or ethical feeling in the eyes, in the set of the jaw, in the glowering expression of pure malicious *hate*, portraits of *one* man. Carl could, we know, very well feed people to crocs, no doubt about it.

I find, amazingly enough, that a play-by-play analysis or recital of the never-ending litany of Carl Panzram's crimes and misdemeanors would be a tedious, and pointless excursion (and he is not being paid ten cents a word, either). Suffice it to say, I think you rather get the point. By his thirties, Carl hated everyone and everything; he dealt in pain and blood and death, well on his road to lasting infamy.

It was to prison guard Harry Lesser that he wrote his confessions; Lesser eventually broke the story of Carl's life of destruction to a wider audience, penning a book containing the confessions of the man who read Nietzsche and exuded ill-will from every pore of his body. Lesser, a Jew who might have felt the stigma of his Jewishness in an era before political correctness, goggled at such lines as:

> In my lifetime I have murdered 21 human beings, I have committed thousands of burglaries, robberies, larcenies, arsons and, last but not

> least, I have committed sodomy on more than 1,000 male human beings. For all these things I am not in the least bit sorry.
>
> I don't believe in man, God, nor Devil. I hate the whole damned human race, including myself. I preyed upon the weak, the harmless, and the unsuspecting. This lesson I was taught by others: Might makes right.
>
> I am sorry for only two things. These two things are I am sorry that I have mistreated some few animals in my lifetime, and I am sorry that I am unable to murder the whole damned human race. I wish the entire human race had one neck and I had my hands around it!

Most tellingly, Carl confessed here:

> I sat down to think things over a bit. While I was sitting there, a little kid about eleven or twelve years old came bumming around. He was looking for something. He found it too. I took him out to a gravel pit about one quarter mile away. I left him there, but first committed sodomy on him and then killed him. His brains were coming out of his ears when I left him, and he will never be any deader.

I could go on and on with such quotes, but, really, I think you get the picture.

†

The day was hot; the workers were sweating it out in the laundry. The heavy smell of bleach and stagnant water mixed with the acrid odor of sweat and grime covering the bodies of the inmate employees.

The beetling brow of the foreman seemed a secure target to Carl as he dipped and dunked crusted sheets into the bubbling vats of lye. Inside of himself, he felt the inner craving toward destruction, the lust for murder that had to be slaked. The hateful foreman of the prison laundry was sauntering up and down the aisles, between the wash. Carl clenched and unclenched his fists, his blood singing in his ears.

He felt the light grow dim, the world grow black. He approached the cigar-chomping foreman.

When he struck, it was with the speed and fierce killing intensity of a serpent. His hands closed around the foreman's throat. Carl easily overpowered him.

When they found him, it was with his body hanging from one of the bubbling tubs of filthy wash.

This was Carl's final murderous fling.

"And He Will Never Be Any Deader!"

Sentenced to death.

Not a problem for Carl Panzram. "I don't wish to reform anyone, because the only way I think you can reform anyone is to kill them." Apparently, he also included himself in this assessment.

He rebuffed any suggestion that he should seek a stay of execution.

The day might have been dark and lowering when Carl was led to the scaffold. Unlike Lillian Gish in D. W. Griffith's silent film epic Intolerance, there would be no waif-like flower of maidenhood racing against time to forestall Carl's execution. Even Carl didn't wish to do that.

"Hurry it up, you Hoosier bastard!" spat the murderous misanthrope at the hangman. "I could kill twenty men while you're fiddling with that damn rope!"

Carl fell through the trapdoor, into eternity.

The date was September 9, 1930. Leavenworth, Kansas. Carl was thirty-nine.

CHAPTER 5

Dead Redemption

The Depraved Deeds of Henry Spencer

To most who have ever heard the name, Henry Spencer is the dour, lugubrious somnambulist that shuffles through a nightmare surreality in David Lynch's classic *avant garde* cult pic, Eraserhead. That character was portrayed by the late actor Jack Nance, who may or may not have been murdered on his way back from a Los Angeles donut shop in 1997. (His story to friends was that he was knocked down by two male Hispanics; many thought he may have just been drunk and fallen over. At any rate, he succumbed to his injuries and was found dead in his apartment.)

Whether or not Mr. Lynch was aware of any *other* Henry Spencer when he conceived his bizarre alter-ego with the piled-up hair, is a matter I do not know. I don't suppose anyone has ever asked him. In the years leading up to the First World War, in Wheaton, Illinois . . .

A young man disembarked from the local train station, carrying his luggage in one hand, fading into the shuffling throng of humanity, largely unnoticed and completely unknown. His name was Henry Spencer.

According to an assessment made by a journalist later, he was a "rat, died like a rat." This journalist had a running bet with the famous pre-WWI journalist Ben Hecht. But more about that later.

The young man had disembarked from the train from points unknown. We are uncertain as to his entire history. Who, at this late date, would care to track down such information? Some thorough biographer perhaps, but, for the purposes of this tome, we can begin where the case truly begins.

The young man was blonde. Bespectacled. Altogether, he was soft-spoken—charming, yet somewhat bland. Most women of the period would have taken him for handsome, if not especially prepossessing. He lugged his case with him from the station. He would, most likely, put up at a rooming house.

"A little place with bugs in the bedsprings," he laughed to himself. "A place where a dowdy old spinster serves up cold mush in the morning, with coffee like mud. A place where everyone is in bed by eight. And, of course, no girls allowed . . ."

This last pained him a little. He had plans to do a little romancing while in town.

†

It was to this end that he began to court the young, attractive dancing teacher Miss Rexroat. The young woman found herself quite taken with Mr. Spencer, who invited her on a fateful, fatal picnic.

†

The day might have been sunny. Must have been bright, idyllic. The flies buzzed around the food. Henry leaned far back in the lap of Miss Rexroat.

"Gee," he said, "A fellow sure could get used to this sort of treatment." He looked wistfully up at the clouds.

"Just don't get too comfortable," she reminded him. "I can't have you falling asleep on me. I mean, you still have to drive us home."

He groaned, rolled over a little, out of her lap, and picking himself up, dusted off his trousers and walked behind her, working himself up to his next act. Concealed about his person was a hammer. How he had managed to keep her from realizing he had secreted away such an item was a mystery in and of itself. At any rate, she was staring wistfully off into the sunset, a fly somnolently buzzing around her pretty ear.

Her ear.

Her ear.

Her pretty, pretty ear, he thought madly.

He raised the piece of iron and wood into the air. It was one moment in time, frozen forever, this act of horror and madness. He brought the hammer down with a killing intensity. She did not scream—would that have alerted any passersby, if there had been any in the immediate vicinity? He supposed it would have. Blood spattered the clean, checked cloth as she slumped over silently, falling like a piece of wood onto her face. He heaved and gasped above her, his heart hammering in his chest, his body rigid, his lust for violence sated.

He threw the hammer down. There was some blood on his clothing, spatters and droplets—and, he had to get rid of the hammer. Bury it in the bushes. They'd never find him out, by God.

He left the body a mess.

†

They did, indeed, "find him out."

It was short work actually. The bank teller became suspicious, as Mr. Spencer claimed himself as the sole recipient of Ms. Rexroat's savings. "That's an awful lot of money to be drawing out at one time, feller," said the suspicious old man, eyeing the suspicious young man, suspiciously. He fancied, as he bent low on the other side of the cage that, eventually, this young man would himself be staring out from behind a set of heavy metal bars. And he was not wrong.

The police were alerted. The young man took his blood money to the train station, waiting nervously for the 1 p.m. "flyer." The sheriff and his deputy collared him there; he was taken into custody, brought back to the city jail, and thrown in the slammer.

The bland, mild-looking young man simply shrugged his shoulders. Was he his brother's (sister's?) keeper? How in the world should he know where Miss Rexroat was?

A local farmer (history does not give the name; at least, not in the account I've read) had seen the couple picnicing—on his property. He quickly led law enforcement on a hunt to find the missing Miss. And they eventually, of course, did.

The shallow grave was exhumed.

Mr. Spencer had a lot of explaining to do.

"I confess!" the bland-looking young man might have said, bent over in prostrate, emotional agony of release as the stern coppers stared him down. "I killed her! I smashed in her head with a hammer. Did it for the life savings. Was planning on skipping out with it! Oh, I killed her all right! God forgive me, I'm the guilty man!" (Not a literal transcription, but you rather get the point.)

It was the work of a few hours for him to lead Wheaton police on a search for the blood-caked hammer. He located it rather quickly.

Even more quickly (or so it must have seemed to him), he was sentenced to hang. Up until the point when he would walk out onto the gallows, he was treated with rather kid gloves by his captors. A photo reproduced in Bloodletters and Badmen shows him having a catered dinner with the detectives in his cell. He looks up at the cameras; his bespectacled eyes, carefully parted hair, and inscrutable, semi-ovoid face not for an instant betraying what possessed him to bring that hammer down on the pretty, doomed head of Miss Rexroat. Apparently, he had never committed such a foul, unconscionable act before.

In truth, we know next to nothing about the family background or past life of this mysterious, monstrous young man. What we do know is that he found "salvation" quite late in life, with the shadow of the noose looming.

"I'm a changed man, forgiven by the grace of God almighty and my savior, Jesus Christ!" said the young man, who altogether reminded one of a store clerk. He was often, these days, found bent at his bunk in his cell, in the company of the pious missionaries the McAuslins, his spiritual advisers.

"The Bible says: ask and ye shall be forgiven. Knock and it shall be answered unto thee. Seek and ye shall find . . .well, I've made a mess of this life, but I am seeking. And I believe I have found. When I go to my death, it will be as one who has found peace and redemption, safe in the bosom of the Lord."

But, some cynical men can perhaps be forgiven for having their doubts. An enterprising pair of reporters, one of them reportedly the famous Ben

Hecht (all I know of him is that he wrote a tag line for *Gone With the Wind* that ended, " . . . For it is but a dream remembered. A civilization . . . gone with the wind." I heard this in a video , read by Satanist Anton LaVey, a man who would certainly have understood the sort of dark, buried monsters of the human psyche that drove Henry Spencer to commit his own foul act of homicide.)

"It's all a pious act," proclaimed Hecht's colleague rather loudly. "Spencer's a rat, and he'll die like a rat. You just wait and see."

Indeed, the two men had a sort of bet going. Would Spencer crack under the pressure of his own impending death? Would chips begin to show through the holy-holy facade? They would just have to wait and see.

They didn't have long to wait.

It was the next day, with Smith, Hecht's friend, laying "three-to-one" against the rat, Spencer (who was, according to Smith, "Providing his own hop. He's scared pissless, and he's found something to keep his knees from buckling on the gallows's steps."). Hecht, rather out of character, believed that Henry was sincere; Smith kept up his assertion that Spencer would die like a rat.

Other reporters joined in the betting pool. That next day, as judgment loomed, huge crowds turned out with picnic baskets, balloons, and little tots in tow, all to see the rat take his punishment.

Spencer is quoted, by that august personage Jay Robert Nash, as having said, "*He* knows me. I am a brand snatched from the burning. I have repented. My soul is washed of all wickedness. God can look into it and see that there is nothing evil left. That's why He will let me into heaven. Because there is not a single lie in me—only truth!"

However, once he actually ascended the gallows, it became a far different story; Christian courage faltered, his hopes of salvation might have seemed dim; might have seemed, to him at least, as if they had been "dashed against the rocks." He suddenly broke out into a bitter, lying harangue, his last testament to the world.

"What I got to say is that I'm innocent of the murder of Allison Rexroat! I never killed her! It's a lie! You're all dirty bastards! You got no right! I never touched her! So help me God, I never harmed a hair on her head! So help me God!"

(He had already freely confessed to the murder.)

"He died just like a rat!" said Mr. Hecht's colleague. "What did I tell you?"

Needless to say, Ben Hecht was a wee bit more cynical after that particular episode.

CHAPTER 6

Ghosts of Deadwood

Outlaws, Gunslingers, and the Killing of Wild Bill Hickok

It's said that Wild Bill had a premonition about his own death.

He somehow knew that Deadwood, South Dakota, would be the final stop on his journey through this life, that he would meet his *mea culpa* in the rough and tumble frontier outpost. How this would come about, specifically, it does not say he knew. He may, for all we know, have seen the thing in a dream.

One fine day, while playing five-card draw with some other hard hombres in a saloon, Wild Bill found himself sitting with his back to the door. In the ancient Norse Havamal (followed today by practicers of the religion of Asatru), the warrior is entreated to never sit with his back to a door—as this, of course, invites danger, invites an enemy to attack him from his vulnerable side. Typically, Wild Bill would not have sat thusly, but, on this specific occasion, after asking one of the gentleman with which he was playing if he would change seats with him, and being completely rebuffed, Wild Bill relented and continued his game. It was, alas, a game he was going to lose.

He had the "Dead Man's Hand": two aces and two eights. The fifth card had already been disposed of, and there is some dispute as to what, specifically, that card might have been. What do you think that card might have been?

A man named McCall strode through the doors of the Nutall and Mann Saloon there in dusty, deadly Deadwood. The previous day, he had lost a considerable amount of money to Wild Bill, who, tossing him a few dollars, suggested he go and get something to eat with it. This was, most decidedly, the wrong thing to tell Mr. McCall (who, incidentally, was known locally as "Crooked Nose Jack"), who took no small umbrage at what he saw as definite condescension on the part of Mr. Hickok.

Mr. McCall came through the (we may assume, or at the least, envision) bat-wing doors of the saloon, like something from a silent Western, and, as if he were gunning for William S. Hart or Tom Mix, strode up to the redoubtable Wild Bill, and, brandishing his Colt .45 firearm, exclaimed, "Here! Take that!"

He then blew Mr. Hickok a lead love letter. It punctured his head, flew out his cheek, and struck another man in the wrist. Wild Bill hit the floor; attempts to revive him were mainly unsuccessful, as he was killed almost instantly.

Mr. McCall's motives for the killing remained obscure. When they hanged him, they cut him down and put him in his cheap pine casket with the noose still hanging from his neck.

The date of the killing was August 1, 1876.

Crooked Nose Jack was hanged for it after two separate trials. (The "double jeopardy" clause usually invoked here was felt not to apply, as Deadwood was considered a hostile entity deep within Indian territory, and its status as part of the federal United States was, at the time, a matter of conjecture.)

†

Even today, there is a certain mystique about the Old West, about sagebrush, arroyo, tumbleweeds, clapboard buildings, gunslingers . . . and of course, their victims. It was a simpler, more majestic time, we assume: a time when women were women and men were ruthless killers. Or, alternately, ran like yellow dogs from the encroaching posse.

We might, for a moment, visualize the dusty, rough-and-tumble town of Deadwood as the set of some ancient Western epic, perhaps from the silent era. Maybe Mack Sennett would let Mabel Normand direct. More likely, it would be Thomas Ince directing William S. Hart in some cattle opera with wildly gesticulating silent-era actors and actresses in too much pancake makeup. The reality may not have been far removed from this Hollywood image.

The dancing girls a certain Mr. Swearengen "recruited" from the rank and file applicants, culled from the naive farms and little, middling burgs of the Midwest, were brought to the mining camp with false promises—not unlike the runaway teens who find themselves captive to pornographers and pimps after false promises of Hollywood stardom. These girls, upon getting off the train, were soon made aware of exactly what was expected of them—to their horror and indignation, of course.

Girls who resisted were threatened. Beaten. If they continued to resist, Swearengen could turn them out-of-doors: that is, leave them solitary women to fend for themselves in a rough and lawless mining town. Here, alone, they stood little chance. They starved. Some committed suicide, becoming the forlorn, forgotten female spirits of Deadwood.

No; most realized, soon, that it was better to become one of the painted hussies, the "comfort women" who flitted through the old Swearengen theater, than to challenge Swearengen openly, or try to make it on their own in rough Deadwood, an unforgiving place for women unattached and unemployed. Destitution, under such circumstances, was imminent.

Death could strike at the most inopportune of times, under the strangest of circumstances. Mr. Hickok soon realized this, as well as many other men. To give an example, one man, making himself a boorish, barbarous drunken oaf in a local saloon, was soon treated to both barrels of a double ought six. His brains blew out the back of his head (and, I must assume, all over the card players, drunks, whores, and piano player) and, to quote again Carl Panzram, "He will never be any deader."

The killer? A dusty, exhausted barmaid tired of his unwanted sexual advances. (Who says women are the "weaker sex"?)

Incidentally, one of the dubious loves of Wild Bill's life, the outlaw mistress Calamity Jane, was reputedly infatuated with Hickok. Jane, not a shirking little flower, she was a large, masculine, muscular woman with tawny, leathery, weather-beaten skin, an unappealing face, and a penchant for wearing mens' clothing. Which, considering the time period, made her stand out a wee bit from the rest of the gals.

But, my friends, she shot straight and true.

The Heroine of the Plains

Born on May Day in 1851, Martha Jane Canary's mother died when she was still a little girl, prompting her father to pick up and move her and her siblings (three brothers and two sisters) from Princeton, Missouri, to Virginia and, finally, to Salt Lake City, Utah. It was here that he died, and Martha Jane took control of her younger brothers and sisters, leading her family by taking any job she could find, doing time as a dishwasher, cook, ox-team driver, and, occasionally, prostitute. She eventually pulled up stakes, and took her brood of orphaned kinfolk to Fort Laramie, Wyoming, where her rough-and-tumble, hardscrabble existence as "one of the boys" began in earnest.

Much valued for her beauty (which, depending on your personal taste in women, didn't last long) "Calamity" Jane described a life, later, that could have been penned by Louis Lamour or Zane Grey. How much of it is actually true, and how much of it personally-spun legend to entertain visitors to Buffalo Bill's Wild West Show is a matter of conjecture. Whatever the case, by 1872, the twenty-one-year-old part-time prostitute, part-time cowpuncher, was busily battling Indian insurgencies on the Great Plains.

Her description of how she acquired her legendary nickname was as follows:

In '72, riding out to Quell, an Indian uprising (one in which six of their soldiers had been killed), Jane's commanding officer, a chap name Captain Egan, was hit in an ambush. Jane, looking back, saw him tottering on the saddle, as if about to fall. Racing back to assist him, she caught him in the nick of time, dashing back to the fortified encampment with bullets and arrows whizzing about her, like a real-life character out of a television Western of the 1950s . . .

Or maybe not.

It was denied by certain august personages that Jane ever, in her life, saw action on the Indian frontier, or served under any military regiment. Instead, she was reviled as a "dissolute, devilish character," but one who often managed to win the hearts of friends and neighbors through her untrammeled generosity.

(It was likewise said that she actually acquired her name through a ribald joke: i.e., to court Jane was, indeed, a "calamity" for any man.)

Jane was said to have swum a raging river with dispatches for Indian fighters, to have convalesced for weeks afterward, ill, and finally to have joined a wagon train headed to . . . Deadwoood. In the 1876 *Deadwood Register* it was reported: "Calamity Jane has Arrived!" This was the same wagon train carrying her inamorata, the slain lawman "Wild" Bill Hickok, whom we have already discussed.

Jane, up to her old tricks, worked the tough-as-nails town of Deadwood as an occasional prostitute (again, depending on your taste, either a welcoming or slightly frightening proposition). All the while, she became increasingly smitten with Hickok; we do not know how the affections were returned, or if they indeed were.

Most likely they were simply "blood brothers."

(On the other hand, a woman claiming to be "Jean Hickok Burkhardt McCormick" later came forth claiming to be the daughter of Hickok and Canary. She made the astonishing revelation that Jane and Hickok had actually married in Montana in September of 1873. Her evidence were the letters her mother had allegedly sent her, which were later published in a book. She further claimed that her mother had given her up for adoption to a "Captain O'Neill." This, of course, can never be verified.)

Jane's actual offspring, which seem to have been two daughters, suffered under her predilection for doing whatever the hell she felt like when she felt like it. A charity fundraiser to send her oldest daughter to an educational institution reportedly ended badly, with Calamity Jane getting drunk and squandering the money (card playing?) that same night, then taking her daughter and riding out of town. Presumably with a massive hangover and a little regret.

(Actually, scratch that last one. If there is one thing we *cannot* imagine Calamity Jane feeling, it is an ounce of regret.)

Some said Hickok had "no use" for Jane while she was alive; but, of course, this matters little to the love-struck. Jane claimed that, so stricken was she by Hickok's murder by McCall, that she went after the varlet with a "meat cleaver." (Where were her famous guns?)

Probably not true. Probably a part of the legend Jane, the Dime Museum attraction, was already spinning around herself. It was the legend that would see penny dreadful authors use her as a fictional heroine.

Jane was thought to be functionally illiterate. Thus, this Dime Museum pamphlet, reprinted here, was almost certainly written by someone else. "Jane" gives a full, wildly inauthentic but nonetheless amusing account of her rootin' tootin' shootin' lifestyle:

Life and Adventures of Calamity Jane

By Herself

My maiden name was Marthy Cannary. I was born in Princeton, Missouri, May 1, 1852. Father and Mother were natives of Ohio. I had two brothers and three sisters, I being the oldest of the children. As a child I always had a fondness for adventure and outdoor exercise and especial fondness for horses, which I began to ride at an early age and continued to do so until I became an expert rider being able to ride the most vicious and stubborn of horses, in fact the greater portion of my life in early times was spent in this manner.

In 1865, we emigrated from our homes in Missouri by the overland route to Virginia City, Montana, taking five months to make the journey. While on the way the greater portion of my time was spent in hunting along with the men and hunters of the party; in fact, I was at all times with the men when there was excitement and adventures to be had. By the time we reached Virginia City, I was considered a remarkable good shot and a fearless rider for a girl of my age. I remember many occurrences on the journey from Missouri to Montana. Many times in crossing the mountains the conditions of the trail were so bad that we frequently had to lower the wagons over ledges by hand with ropes for they were so rough and rugged that horses were of no use. We also had many exciting times fording streams for many of the streams in our way were noted for quicksands and boggy places, where, unless we were very careful, we would have lost horses and all. Then we had many dangers to encounter in the way of streams swelling on account of heavy rains. On occasions of that kind the men would usually select the best places to cross the streams, myself on more than one occasion have mounted my pony and swam across the stream several times merely to amuse myself and have had many narrow escapes from having both myself and pony washed away to certain death, but as the pioneers of those days had plenty of courage we overcame all obstacles and reached Virginia City in safety.

Mother died at Black Foot, Montana, 1866, where we buried her. I left Montana in Spring of 1866, for Utah, arriving at Salt Lake city during the summer. Remained in Utah until 1867, where my father died, then went to Fort Bridger, Wyoming Territory, where we arrived May 1, 1868, then went to Piedmont, Wyoming, with U.P. Railway. Joined General Custer as a scout at Fort Russell, Wyoming, in 1870, and started for Arizona for the Indian Campaign. Up to this time I had always worn the costume of my sex. When I joined Custer I donned the uniform of a soldier. It was a bit awkward at first, but I soon got to be perfectly at home in men's clothes.

Was in Arizona up to the winter of 1871, and during that time, I had a great many adventures with the Indians, for as a scout I had a great many dangerous missions to perform, and while I was in many close places always succeeded in getting away safely, for by this time I was considered the most reckless and daring rider and one of the best shots in the western country.

After that campaign I returned to Fort Sanders, Wyoming, remained there until spring of 1872, when we were ordered out to the Muscle Shell or Nursey Pursey Indian outbreak. In that war Generals Custer, Miles, Terry, and Crook were all engaged. This campaign lasted until fall of 1873.

It was during this campaign that I was christened Calamity Jane. It was on Goose Creek, Wyoming, where the town of Sheridan is now located. Capt. Egan was in command of the Post. We were ordered out to quell an uprising of the Indians, and were out for several days, had numerous skirmishes during which six of the soldiers were killed and several severely wounded. When on returning to the Post we were ambushed about a mile and a half from our destination. When fired upon Capt. Egan was shot. I was riding in advance and on hearing the firing turned in my saddle and saw the Captain reeling in his saddle as though about to fall. I turned my horse and galloped back with all haste to his side and got there in time to catch him as he was falling. I lifted him onto my horse in front of me and succeeded in getting him safely to the Fort. Capt. Egan on recovering, laughingly said: "I name you Calamity Jane, the heroine of the plains." I have borne that name up to the present time. We were afterwards ordered to Fort Custer, where Custer City now stands, where we arrived in the spring of 1874; remained around Fort Custer all summer and were ordered to Fort Russell in fall of 1874, where we remained until spring of 1875; was then ordered to the Black Hills to protect miners, as that country was controlled by the Sioux Indians, and the government had to send the soldiers to protect the lives of the miners and settlers in that section.

Remained there until fall of 1875 and wintered at Fort Laramie. In spring of 1876, we were ordered north with General Crook to join Gen'ls Miles, Terry, and Custer at Big Horn river. During this march I swam the Platte river at Fort Fetterman as I was the bearer of important dispatches. I had a ninety-mile ride to make, being wet and cold, I contracted a severe illness and was sent back in Gen. Crook's ambulance to Fort Fetterman where I laid in the hospital for fourteen days. When able to ride I started for Fort Laramie where I met Wm. Hickok, better known as Wild Bill, and we started for Deadwood, where we arrived about June.

During the month of June I acted as a pony express rider carrying the U.S. mail between Deadwood and Custer, a distance of fifty miles, over one of the roughest trails in the Black Hills country. As many of the riders before me had been held up and robbed of their packages, mail, and money that they carried, for that was the only means of getting mail and money between these points.

It was considered the most dangerous route in the Hills, but as my reputation as a rider and quick shot was well known, I was molested very little, for the toll gatherers looked on me as being a good fellow, and they knew that I never missed my mark. I made the round trip every two days, which was considered pretty good riding in that country. Remained around Deadwood all that summer visiting all the camps within an area of one hundred miles.

My friend, Wild Bill, remained in Deadwood during the summer with the exception of occasional visits to the camps. On the 2nd of August, while setting at a gambling table in the Bell Union saloon, in Deadwood, he was shot in the back of the head by the notorious Jack McCall, a desperado. I was in Deadwood at the time and on hearing of the killing made my way at once to the scene of the shooting and found that my friend had been killed by McCall. I at once started to look for the assassin and found him at Shurdy's butcher shop and grabbed a meat cleaver and made him throw up his hands; through the excitement on hearing of Bill's death, having left my weapons on the post of my bed.

He was then taken to a log cabin and locked up, well secured as every one thought, but he got away and was afterwards caught at Fagan's ranch on Horse Creek, on the old Cheyenne road and was then taken to Yankton, Dak., where he was tried, sentenced, and hung.

I remained around Deadwood locating claims, going from camp to camp until the spring of 1877, where one morning, I saddled my horse and rode towards Crook city. I had gone about twelve miles from Deadwood, at the mouth of Whitewood Creek, when I met the overland mail running from Cheyenne to Deadwood. The horses on a run, about 200 yards from the station; upon looking closely I saw they were pursued by Indians. The horses ran to the barn as was their custom.

As the horses stopped I rode along side of the coach and found the driver John Slaughter, lying face downwards in the boot of the stage, he having been shot by the Indians. When the stage got to the station the Indians hid in the bushes. I immediately removed all baggage from the coach except the mail. I then took the driver's seat and with all haste drove to Deadwood, carrying the six passengers and the dead driver.

I left Deadwood in the fall of 1877, and went to Bear Butte Creek with the 7th Cavalry. During the fall and winter we built Fort Meade and the town of Sturgis. In 1878, I left the command and went to Rapid City and put in the year prospecting.

In 1879, I went to Fort Pierre and drove trains from Rapid city to Fort Pierre for Frank Witc, then drove teams from Fort Pierce to Sturgis for Fred Evans. This teaming was done with oxen as they were better fitted for the work than horses, owing to the rough nature of the country.

In 1881, I went to Wyoming and returned in 1882 to Miles City and took up a ranch on the Yellow Stone, raising stock and cattle, also kept a way side inn, where the weary traveler could be accommodated with food, drink, or trouble if he looked for it. Left the ranch in 1883, went to California, going through the States and territories, reached Ogden the latter part of 1883, and San Francisco in 1884. Left San Francisco in the summer of 1884 for Texas, stopping at Fort Yuma, Arizona, the hottest spot in the United States. Stopping at all points of interest until I reached El Paso in the fall. While in El Paso, I met Mr. Clinton Burk, a native of Texas, who I married in August 1885. As I thought I had travelled through life long enough alone and thought it was about time to take a partner for the rest of my days.

We remained in Texas leading a quiet home life until 1889. On October 28, 1887, I became the mother of a girl baby, the very image of its father, at least that is what he said, but who has the temper of its mother.

When we left Texas we went to Boulder, Colo., where we kept a hotel until 1893, after which we travelled through Wyoming, Montana, Idaho, Washington, Oregon, then back to Montana, then to Dakota, arriving in Deadwood October 9, 1895, after an absence of seventeen years.

My arrival in Deadwood after an absence of so many years created quite an excitement among my many friends of the past, to such an extent that a vast number of the citizens who had come to Deadwood during my absence who had heard so much of Calamity Jane and her many adventures in former years were anxious to see me.

Among the many whom I met were several gentlemen from eastern cities who advised me to allow myself to be placed before the public in such a manner as to give the people of the eastern cities an opportunity of seeing the Woman Scout who was made so famous through her daring career in the West and Black Hill countries.

An agent of Kohl and Middleton, the celebrated Museummen came to Deadwood, through the solicitation of the gentleman who I had met there and arrangements were made to place me before the public in this manner. My first engagement began at the Palace Museum, Minneapolis, January 20, 1896, under Kohl and Middleton's management.

Hoping that this little history of my life may interest all readers, I remain as in the older days,

Yours,
Mrs. M. Burk
Better Known As Calamity Jane

†

Jane passed into that great big arroyo in the sky on August 1, 1903. She had tried unsuccessfully to live the settled life of a rancher and an innkeeper. Sadly, her addiction to alcohol ended that badly.

She married a man named Burk and had a daughter, Jane, who was given up for adoption. It was reported that, at this point, she was so alcoholic that the best she could do in life was washing and cooking for a whorehouse madam and her girls.

Jane traveled by train to Terry, a small town not far from Deadwood, and was so drunk, reportedly, she had to be carried off the train. She died at the Calloway Hotel a few hours later of pneumonia and stomach inflammation. She was fifty-one. Among her few possessions were found a passel of unsent letters to her daughter.

She was buried in Mount Moriah Cemetery in Deadwood, next to Wild Bill Hickok. So denied their true romance in life, they at least enjoy each other's company in eternal repose.

In pace requiescat.

As a final note, I've decided to add a Western legend we adapted some time back, about one of Calamity Jane's old traveling companions, outlaw Sam Bass. Who was a Texan, incidentally.

Sam Bass Snares the Detective

Once, Sam Bass and his gang caught wind of the fact that a notorious detective was on their trail. The detective might have been a Pinkerton, or he might not have; the story doesn't relate.

At any rate, Sam was driving his wagon one day, carefully hidden beneath a low hood, like an old peasant woman. He might have been a strange sight, but to the young man stranded (due to losing a wheel block on his own carriage), the sight of Sam coming along that road must have been mighty welcome.

Sam asked the man, politely enough, what he was doing all the way out here in the woods. The man answered, "I've come to seek out and kill Sam Bass."

Sam shook his head, smiled. Then he said, "And would you know Sam Bass if you saw him?"

To which the detective replied simply, "No."

Sam cracked a huge grin, leaned over, pulled down his hood, and said, "Well, you're riding with him right now!"

The detective suddenly lost a great deal of his bluster and courage. He began to whine and weep, begging for his life on behalf of his wife and child.

Sam, being the big-hearted desperado that he was, let the man off with just a warning never to show his face around those parts again.

And the bold detective never did.

(Source: Popular American folklore.)

†

Once, there was a land of dry, dusty trails, tumbleweeds and tough-as-leather hombres known as the Old West. In countless frontier boom towns, snake-eyed desperados lived and died, throwing up their shooting irons and casting their long shadows in the burning fires of an unforgiving sunset. Can you hear them down at the local saloon, singing hosannas over cheap whiskey, plumed in cigar smoke, surrounded by bar maids and painted hussies, laying down their poker hands under steely eyes, as nimble fingers work lawlessly at the worn, cracking holsters at their hips?

Somebody coming up the boardwalk, throwing open the batwing doors. Is it Clint Eastwood or Bat Masterton?

After more than a century of time, who can now say?

CHAPTER 7

The Gruesome Mr. Gein

Another Take on the Timeless Terror Tale!

Ed Gein has gained a sort of lasting, infamous notoriety as the single individual whose crimes have inspired more bad movies than anyone else, save for Jack the Ripper. He was, admittedly, the inspiration for Norman Bates, the dress-wearing, mommy-fixated Freudian freako from Alfred Hitchcock's classic movie Psycho (based upon the book by Robert Bloch). Ed also inspired the leather-faced loonies in Tobe Hooper's Texas Chainsaw Massacre films, the dual characters of Hannibal Lecter and Buffalo Bill in Silence of the Lambs, and numerous adaptations of his own sordid saga in countless comic books, movies, and even collector cards. Ed is a sort of celebrity necrophiliac. We're certain that, if he were alive today, he'd have his own reality program. Not too shabby for an obscure little man from Plainfield, Wisconsin, who most likely died a virgin.

Ed was born roundabout the year 1906 to George and Augusta Gein. His mother, as if anyone needed any reminding, was a religious zealot who obsessed over the evils of women and inculcated a deep fear of Hell and the "Whore of Babylon" in both of her young sons (Ed's brother Henry included).

She did this by forcing them to listen as she read from Revelations and by forbidding them to have much of anything in the way of social interaction. They were both expected to tolerate the stultifying drudgery of farm life with no reprieve, no safety-valve, no education in the ways of the wicked world.

As she aged, Augusta became more and more tyrannical, controlling—more of a religious fanatic. Obsessed with the perceived sin of sexual congress in general (and the sexual chastity of her sons in particular), Augusta reportedly began to lose interest in the pathetic, often drunkenly volatile George, who, at any rate, died quite unexpectedly in 1947.

This left Augusta alone with her two boys—one of which, Henry, had had just about enough of the suffocating drudgery of his lot in life, and was, according to legend, getting ready to flee the coop. This must have unaccountably troubled Augusta, and, in turn, troubled the devoted thirty-four-year-old son, Ed.

Henry was unexpectedly killed in a brush fire, while out with Ed. The exact circumstances of his death are peculiarly suspicious. Did Ed coax his brother into a circle of burning trees out of spite for his brother's plan to "desert" the little family? Who knows?

At any rate, Ed now had Augusta all to himself. Both of them lived out the remainder of their marginal existences in a lonely old farmhouse where the wind wailed, the moon glowered, and (we may be reasonably certain) ghosts walked the creaking floorboards at all hours of the night. (Ah, the poeticism of our romantic vision.)

†

Ed was just a little boy when the idea of macabre butchery and death first crystallized itself in his mind. An apocryphal tale goes something like this:

The Geins ran a little store on Main Street, a down-at-the-heels small-town grocery where they doubled as butchers. Ed (and presumably Henry) was forbidden to look in the room in back, where George and Augusta both helped in the slaughtering of animals and the cutting of fresh meat.

But, damn it, Ed did it anyway.

The little boy must have crept over to the door one boring, interminable day, and slowly opened it. Just a peek inside, he thought, to satisfy his curiosity. Of course, like Bluebeard's luckless wife, his curiosity cost him greatly.

He was astounded by the image of his parents—particularly his mother—clothed in dripping leather aprons, pulling the flesh from the body of a freshly-killed hog that was hanging suspended by a hook in the ceiling. Ed recoiled; but was filled, we must assume, with a curious mixture of loathing, fascination . . . and weird, forbidden arousal. A psychologist might be able to tell you what sorts of neural associations the wildly schizophrenic Ed (who beyond having a sinister "sleepy eye" was, reportedly, given to laugh at the most inappropriate moments) must have gained from seeing his sainted mother covered in blood and a leather apron, pulling the muscles and flesh off of a butchered pig . . . but I'm certain we can't.

It was not long before trouble began to plague Ed's peculiar paradise. Augusta suffered a series of strokes and died. Ed was alone, teetering on the brink of sanity.

He began to formulate a wall between himself and his past, the outside world, delving deeper and deeper into the macabre kingdom of his own fantasies and fixations, closing off Augusta's bedroom and keeping it in pristine, virginal condition. The rest of the decrepit house fell into sordid squalor.

Ed began to obsessively collect sensational popular magazines, mostly featuring subjects of murder, crime, and "true detection." He also liked books on Nazi atrocities (think: lamp shades made from human skin, ashtrays made from pelvic bones, that sort of thing), as well as books on anatomy, embalming, funeral customs . . . pleasant bathroom reading, to be sure.

Ed subsisted on cans of pork and beans, heated directly in their can on the stove. He did odd jobs, sold his fields, and even babysat (the reader is forgiven a shudder at the thought). Of course, some of the local children began to gossip that Fast Eddie had shown them "shrunken heads" he claimed a relative had sent him from the South Pacific during the war.

Ed was also courting. Or, at the least, was making a rather comic attempt to do so. He was interested in middle- aged women who looked like his mother; no surprise there. One such woman was a buxom, foul-mouthed barmaid named Mary Hogan.

(Note: During the ensuing ten years after all of Ed's close relations died, a number of peculiar disappearances, most notably that of a babysitter named Weckler, occurred in close proximity. It has been suggested that Ed may very well have perpetrated these murders. If so, he never confessed to doing so.)

There was also talk that the grounds around Ed's house were haunted—by the mysterious apparition of a woman with long flowing hair. The titular ghost was said to cavort madly near the moonlit road. There may, in point of fact, have been some truth to this.

Mary Hogan disappeared in 1954, leaving only a trail of blood at her workplace. It would be three long years before another middle-aged woman, the hardware store owner Bernice Worden, would also mysteriously vanish.

It was November 16 of 1957 to be exact, and two eyewitnesses had seen a funny little man go into Bernice Worden's store the day she came up missing—a little fellow that bore a striking resemblance to the Elmer Fudd-like Eddie Gein. Bloodstains were found in the store; the cash register was missing.

Sheriff Shley went to hunt down Ed. He found him having dinner with some friends in town. (More likely, they were less "friends" than folks that felt a certain amount of pity for the lonely, eccentric little man.)

When confronted by the lawmen, Ed slipped up badly, said, "If someone is pointing the finger at me being responsible for the kidnapping of Bernice Worden, they're trying to frame me!" This made the policemen mighty suspicious, as they had yet to even tell Ed why they were there.

The rest, of course, is horrifying history. Ed was taken in for questioning. Meanwhile, the sheriff and his deputies went out to the Gein homestead. What they found out there would haunt them (or anyone else who was unlucky enough to actually see it) to their dying days.

The headless body of Bernice Worden was trussed up, like a deer, in a disused shed, hanging upside down. She had been decapitated, and was split from her groin to her neck.

As if this hideous discovery was not enough, the officers that ventured into the macabre filth of the decayed Gein farmhouse also discovered Ed's grisly collection of sick relics, the products of his demented craftsmanship and grave robbing excursions.

These included:

• A knife with a handle of human bone.
• Skulls on the bedposts.
• Lamp shades covered in human skin.
• Human lips on a drawstring.
• A heart in a sauce pan.
• Leggings made from female skin.
• A torso with strings made from a female corpse.
• Several "skin masks" (some lovingly oiled to preserve their flexibility) with lipstick applied. These were obviously made to wear.
• A rocker with human femur bones for armrests.
Bernice Worden's severed head with nails hammered into it.
• Various fleshy odds and ends.

The lawmen were physically sick. Ed became an overnight psycho celebrity.

In the wake of the ghoulish discoveries, jokes began to circulate—"Geiners," so named because they poked what seemed like harmless fun at the hideous doings of the Plainfield maniac. Not only that, but Ed's car (in which he presumably transported the bodies he exhumed from Plainfield Cemetery, as well as his two living victims) was bought and put on tour!

The farmhouse itself burned to the ground quite mysteriously. Arson was suspected. (But, if it was local residents who committed the arson, could they really be blamed?)

Ed was found unfit to stand trial. He was committed to the Wisconsin State Hospital for the Criminally Insane, where he died July 26, 1984. Further examination by psychiatrists over the years yielded interesting information, such as Ed's off-the-cuff answer to the old saying, "A bird in the hand is worth two in the bush."

Ed replied, "If you have a bird in your hand, you might squeeze it too hard, and kill it."

CHAPTER 8

Highway to Hell

Interstate Killer Larry Eyler

A despicable human being, Larry Eyler never knew, in the short span of years allotted to him, many happy days. It was a cruel, besotted fate that birthed him in 1952, and it was this happenstance of fate the punishing rewards of which he was to spread, like a rancid layer of congealing blood, across the width and breadth of five states.

Larry traveled the highways and backroads of rural America—killing young gay men. Larry himself, like John Wayne Gacy before him, would struggle against the more constrictive social confines of the late 1900s in an effort to come to grips with his own homosexuality. It was a battle he would not only lose, but one that would go horribly, desperately far wrong.

His face betrays not a little of the look of a devious, bad, and not overly intelligent boy—a mischievous lout; his eyes, in his photographs, seem shifted away from the camera (considering the heinous crimes he was convicted for, this may be only a matter of nature). His look is undeniably boyish; youngish he seems, to the casual observer, like a young man arrested in the line of his development. Curly hair and a thinish moustache seem to add to the notion that he is desperately trying to hide the insecurity that comes with a lack of maturity.

Young gay men began to be found in rural areas—their mutilated bodies showed signs of torture. The MO was not immediately apparent, so the police had little to go on. Crisscrossing what seemed a large area of the Midwest, the bound and gagged cadavers showed signs of sexual torture—the killings had been perpetrated, variously, by stabbing and strangling. Victims ranged in age from nineteen down to fourteen, and the bodies were turning up in places as geographically distant as Lexington, Kentucky, Lowell, Indiana, and Joliet, Illinois.

It seemed that there was a transient sex killer—a man targeting gay men, roaming about the highways and backroads of the Midwest, kidnapping these young gay men and preying upon what might best be described as a vulnerable demographic, because of the then more ready intolerance and lack of understanding as to differences in sexual orientation.

Of course, unbeknownst to police, the killer was the rather boyishly charming Eyler, whose friends described him as a young man with a tempestuous temper lurking beneath a superficially charming exterior.

A young man named Craig Townsend found himself fortunate to survive the kidnapping and assault of the detestable Eyler. Treated at a hospital, the twenty-one-year-old man decided to abandon the police to their investigation, leaving the hospital like a thief in the night, perhaps afraid that turning his evidence over to the authorities might invite the retribution of his attacker.

The Christmas of 1982 brought a trio of Yuletide terrors to rural Indiana, as Eyler found himself a sickening Santa, delivering dead bodies up in the form of three young men trussed-up and killed as before, abandoned like the husks of moldering bugs he had smashed out of life—left to fester on rural routes, to draw flies.

Those killings were perpetrated on or around December 25 and 28, the last being an amazing "twofer"; or, as put in Jack the Ripper parlance, a "Double Event."

Eyler had been apprehended during one such abduction by a nosy authority, a State Highway Patrol officer. At this point, Mr. Eyler had racked up a body count of around twelve, most mutilated, disemboweled; apparently, the frustrated rage of the bitter, self-hating gay man knew no boundaries. (Or perhaps he simply got his cookies off seeing others suffer. Perhaps this was the only way he could achieve an orgasm.)

The officer drove by and saw the truck parked mysteriously near some sparse woods. He then saw a man, identified as Mr. Eyler, escorting another man, who appeared to be bound and gagged, toward a nearby stand of trees. When confronted, the young man, in what seems an almost comic sort of understatement, said that he felt Mr. Eyler was going to perpetrate a "sexual assault" against him. Mr. Eyler did some quick talking, perhaps quickly explaining the situation away with his own smooth, oily charm, as some kinky sex play.

At any rate, while he was now within the radar of law enforcement, he was not at that point taken into custody. Why, we cannot be sure. It seems it would have taken an *awful* lot of persuasion on Eyler's part to explain away rape and kidnapping.

A search of his pickup later revealed clothesline, surgical tape, and a blood-encrusted hunting knife. The blood type matched that of a nineteen-year-old victim named Ralph Calise. (Likewise, tire tracks seemed to match the imprints left by a vehicle near where the body was dumped.) Still, incredibly, police must have felt they didn't have enough.

At any rate, he celebrated his small victory by killing and dismembering more young men. A fourteen-year-old boy from Kenosha, Wisconsin, was next, his mutilated body found, as before, in an abandoned field.

The body count stood at perhaps fifteen or sixteen, reaching a hideous dimension of brutality—four bodies were discovered in Indiana in *one day*. All had been stabbed repeatedly, one decapitated; all had their pants pulled down around their ankles. This was a common facet of Eyler's deplorable perversion, his calling card, as it were.

Even more death would follow. In Indiana, Illinois, and Wisconsin, Eyler would troll the gay scene, looking for victims, looking for the easy prey.

Then, it was mutilation and screaming.

Unbeknownst to the psychopathic monster, however, his own destruction was germinating inside of himself, a fool-proof way for God and biology to repay, with hideous vengeance, the maleficent madness Eyler had been steadily and surely meting out as grim and relentless homicide.

†

By the early 1980s, widespread fear and panic about "gay cancer" was sweeping the nation, religious zealots and conservative pundits using it as a convenient excuse to Bible-thump the masses with sordid pronouncements of Divine Retribution for what they saw as America's Sodomistic descent. As young gay men began to fall prey to the disease, rumor and innuendo flourished, and fear of AIDS soon took center stage alongside fear of communist infiltration and war with Russia (Perhaps not, necessarily, in that order, but you get the idea.)

AIDS made celebrities of some afflicted, like the tragic boy victim Ryan White, while it capped the lives of stars such as Rock Hudson with shocking finality.

Misinformation and grim urban legend filled in the general gaps in human knowledge with tales of lurid fear: What if you could get AIDS from a toilet seat? Or from shaking hands? Deep kissing? Weren't there angry victims, like the legendary "AIDS Mary" going around and infecting people on purpose, or spitting on the vegetables at Safeway?

It was a strangling panic, one reinforced by the grim litany of deaths that, steadily, began to accrue under the steel-fisted domination of the disease.

And this same poisonous snake lay curled, waiting to strike, deep beneath the corrosive skin of killer Larry Eyler. However, he did not know it just then.

†

Larry had a supposed accomplice. The following recreation is an attempt, however sad, to put the reader into the *now* of the event—as if he had actually been there.

Larry sauntered up to the bar, the heavy blare of disco music adding a counterpoint to the thumping of his heart. Several guys sauntered around the dance floor, drunkenly, lazily; the place was a real meat market. That is, if meat, most specifically, was what a man was looking for.

Larry liked his raw.

A young man came over to him, relaxed expression on his face. He sat down on the stool next to Larry, looked over. In the darkness, and with the correct amount of alcohol flowing through his veins, Larry thought most anyone could look like a fucking Adonis. Even himself, who had a boyish, but not astoundingly handsome visage.

"Wow," said Dutch. "You're like wow. I feel like I've seen you somewhere before."

Larry was quiet for a moment. The DJ was spinning a record by some new group from England. Something called "The Cure."

"Yeah, people tell me that. Guess I just have one of those faces, huh?"

Dutch didn't know how to react. Larry looked down at the bulge in his blue jeans. Dutch was . . . all right.

"So, you come in here a lot?"

Larry smiled, tried to thaw. He turned on the charm a little, tip by tap. Trying, always trying to convince.

"Sure. Like you've said, I look like someone you've seen before, right? Guess I just have one of those faces. You know, you can tell a lot by a man based on his appearance."

(Dutch, for instance, thought Larry, had smooth, clean hands and impeccable nails. Obviously not a manual laborer, then. Larry, by contrast, had only ever held grunt jobs [house painter, clerk, etc.]).

"I'm a photographer," he lied, smiling, giving that big grin that always melted them a little. Dutch seemed to take the bait, swiveled on his stool, rested his head on his hand.

He said: "Oh really, how fascinating!" Dutch drew the word fascinating out until it was several syllables: faa—sssscciii-naaa-tiiing. His lips were full; Larry thought they bloomed like a rose.

His breath reeked. His cheekbones were high and tight. Not an ounce of fat on this one, thought Larry. Good eats.

The young man followed Larry out to the parking lot. He was weaving drunkenly, unsteady on his cowboy boots, but Larry helped him, laughing, saying, "Easy partner, easy! You don't want to take a spill out here on the parking lot, do you?"

"No," said Dutch eerily, looking off at the cold row of crime lights that disappeared down the street, at the neon fast-food signs and dirty, run-down strip-mall buildings that looked cold and empty and lifeless at three o'clock in the morning.

"I . . . I don't want to get hurt."

Larry helped him into the cab.

"Sure," he said. He got in the driver's side door, whistling. Anyone who saw him could tell he was perfectly sober.

†

It was cold out here under the stars. His buddy, the "Professor," had his pants down, his pasty, white legs pimpling up into gooseflesh. Larry handled the Polaroid like an expert, hoping nobody would see the flash from the road.

But the quality of the photos was so poor they would have to move to Crime Scene 2. They would take their trussed-up piggie to an abandoned basement—there, maybe they could get better pictures.

The piggie was in and out of consciousness. He was bleeding from his mouth and nose, was moaning slightly, his head lolling drunkenly back and forth.

"Uh . . . hey man, man. I think I'm dyin.'"

Insensate, he thought, quite mistakenly, the two others present might care about this. Later, when they had transported him elsewhere, he would be disabused of this notion. Larry's partner would masturbate furiously as Larry clicked picture after picture, posing the form in the most artificially erotic mannerisms, preserving the fantasies of power and sadistic control.

The Professor had drool dripping from his hamhock chin. His hog leg in his hands, he rasped: "Oh, yeah, put him over there. Yeah, where I can see his ass. Oh, yeah, spread him for me, the little prick, spread him eagle so I can see everything right now." Building to a furious climax, several pasty, glue-like lumps oozed out from between his clenched fingers.

Larry continued to snap away, documenting an event, but, also, collecting nanoseconds of pain like morbid trophies. He could feel his own heart start to pump more furiously, his breath grow ragged. He felt his cock go rigid in his pants, his shaking hands having trouble manipulating the bulky Polaroid camera. Soon, it would be his turn to take his pleasure with the piggie, pull the pants down, expose the sagging balls, the limp, inchworm penis.

Then, the mutilation, the exposure. Then, the screaming would start.

†

Larry Eyler was determined to have his day in court. He would have, as it turned out, many of them, but, for now, he was mostly concerned with suing the Sheriff's Department for what he termed "psychological warfare." In other words, the psychopathic sex slayer was perturbed that the authorities had him under surveillance, their investigation getting closer and closer to uncovering the grim truth of his sordid, sickening existence.

Hence, he had asked the judge to award him half-a-million dollars. Unfortunately for Larry, the court failed to find for him, and he was unceremoniously ejected from the courtroom, right into the waiting arms of officers who placed him under arrest for the murder of Robert Casile.

†

It was the landlord's dog, sniffing about some suspicious garbage sacks in a dumpster out behind Larry's place, that brought to life the sickening crimes of Hell's Highwayman. Larry frequently stayed with his gay lover when he was in Chicago, but also kept an apartment independent of this. On August 21, 1984, the jig was up. The dismembered body of a fifteen-year-old male prostitute was found in several garbage bags—bags that Larry Eyler had recently dumped.

†

The Professor walked due to lack of evidence. What happened to those erotic snaps of the bound and gagged victims? Had Larry taken them himself? If so, what did he do with them?

As part of a plea agreement, Larry agreed to help the police clear up an estimated *twenty* or so killings the Interstate Killer had perpetrated in Illinois, Wisconsin, Indiana, and Michigan. In exchange for this, he would avoid the death penalty—but, ironically, he was working against time.

Inside him, the Three Fates—Clotho, Lachesis, and Atropos—had spun and cut the cord of his worthless existence, consigning him to the death he had so gleefully and sadistically meted out to so many young men. He eventually succumbed to AIDS in 1994, at the age of forty-one.

What he saw in those last days, in the privacy of his own cell, is anyone's guess. Was he meditating on the endless display of cock and balls from mutilated cadavers, left in empty fields, trussed up like animals, stabbed and dismembered for his own personal amusement? Did he think that God was repaying him, blow for blow, scorn for scorn, while he suffocated in the dark, can-like confines of his cell?

We can only guess.

CHAPTER 9

"The Family that Slays Together . . ."

Faye and Ray Copeland

The lonely desolation of a farm is the perfect setting for foul play; all that eerie solitude, far away from the prying eyes of pesky authorities. And miles and miles of land, creeping with hungry critters, the perfect place to dump your victims. (Or maybe, just as Belle Gunness is said to have done, feed them to hungry hogs.)

So imagine if you leased several farms, staffed them with transients. Your hired help are just lonely nobodies, old men that smell like B.O. and cheap hooch. They got nowhere to go, no one to care about them; they are as silent and gray and unloved and unwanted as a bundle of cast-off rags.

And they disappear into the fabric of the world, and are never seen again. Does anyone care? Most likely, no. But murder is murder, after all.

Faye and Ray. A couple with rhyming first names, a man that had known little but hard times since growing up in the dirt and hard-scabble existence of Missouri during the Great Depression. Such an early initiation into the grueling aspects of a punishing life must have taken quite a toll on the young Ray. (Although it is most assuredly a fact that Young Ray grew up in an impoverished family, it is also reported that he was "spoiled" by doting, devoted parents, who lavished on him whatever he wanted. How they managed to afford such extravagances is anyone's guess.)

†

It is recorded that the budding young psychopath first took to robbery and forging checks. This, quite naturally, led into trouble with the authorities. A short stint in a reformatory failed to reform him; but, he eventually learned to keep his dark, hidden, and sadistic side buried deep within his breast. Time etched lines on his face. He married, went to work. His farm became a thriving piece of property.

Somehow, though, his success in life was not enough. He wanted more.

†

The couple kept a ledger. Nimble fingers wrote in the margins of the well-thumbed black book of the couple's doings.

What could those entries have been like?

"Bub Jeffers. Born? Died, just last night. One blow with the hammer, and he was done. Left behind 500 dollars. Good catch."

And why be so specific? This is what would eventually sink the couple.

They had begun to kill their hired help. Ostensibly, this was to rob them, to render them useful even to the point of their own extermination. The lonely little flies were caught by the wings in the comfortable killer web of Faye and Ray's homicidal homestead.

The couple was said to have fashioned a quilt, a nauseating keepsake, from the clothing of the victims. The victims, incidentally, were hired primarily for their ability to purchase cows at auction—with bad checks. Ray Copeland reportedly had already been in a wee bit of trouble with the law for writing such checks. Thus, it was thought expedient to hire clueless vagabonds and vagrants as farm hands, to front for the couple's criminal activities.

Maybe it was five. Maybe twelve. Whatever. Each one disappears into the nameless void of criminal homicide statistics. Each one, apparently, was dispatched unceremoniously with a bullet to the back of the neck. The deaths were recorded, at least five of them, in a ledger, marked with a magic X (bringing to mind Charlie Manson's old saying, "I have Xed myself out of the world!"), and, despite her later claims of absolute clueless innocence, the handwriting indeed belonged to Faye Della Copeland. Their weapon of choice? A .22-caliber Marlin bolt-action rifle, primed and pumped and oiled for killing.

†

Maybe Ray snuck up behind the man was who was pitching hay or tending horses or some damn thing.

Maybe he got him good and drunk first.

"Ain't something I want to do, y'unnerstand? Just some things goes that-a-way, is all."

The man might have put his hands out in a gesture of mercy. Maybe he was calculating the odds of grabbing Ray's gun and using it on him, instead.

"Now, just some things you gotta do. Don't mean you got to like 'em!" Ray might have sounded like Jim Siedow's character in the original Texas Chainsaw Massacre (1974), but we weren't there, and don't have a hotline to God, so must simply shrug.

The wino continued to back into the shadows on the wall. Ray came forward slowly, hefting his rifle, his eyes a blaze, his blood pumping bullets into his brain. His neural synapses were hard-wired to destroy . . .

"Please! No, I'll never tell! I swear. I'll go away, and you'll never see me again! I swear."

Ray spat a chunk of chewing tobacco onto the sod and said, "That's right, you'll never . . ."

Blam!

(The above scenario, a literary digression, is highly unlikely. Most likely, Ray snuck up behind his victims and dispatched them without them ever being the wiser.)

†

The MO here was for the transient to accompany Ray to auction, bid exorbitant prices on cattle, pay with a rubber check, and for Ray to make off like a bandito.

The townfolk had never liked Ray, had never trusted him. Always felt him to be a "menacing oddball," perched just on the edge of some violence. Some even claimed he made roadkill out of stray animals, purposely running the hairy critters down in the street. Local cops had been watching him for years.

His habits of stealing livestock and writing bad checks had been on-again, off-again occupations, but, after marrying the luckless Faye Della , he settled into menial jobs, factory work, and tending his own farm in the off-hours. Grueling, back-breaking labor, labor from which the psychopathic Ray Copeland thought he might have some escape.

†

August 20, 1989, saw an anonymous telephone call into Crime Stoppers. The reporter reportedly reported that Ray and Faye were killing off their hired hands after involving them in financial frauds. Authorities, who, as I mentioned before, had been keeping a wary eye on the elderly, doddering criminal, were not surprised to hear *that* particular name pop up. Perhaps the depth and seriousness of the allegations made did shock them, though.

McCormick, a man describing himself as a common "gutter tramp and drunk," had contacted police with the intention of uncovering the mass murder factory of opportunistic serial killer Ray.

McCormick, Jimmie, had been living at the Victory Mission in Springfield when Ray came calling, tempting the man with promises of $20,000 a year—which, for a fifty-six-year-old "gutter tramp" must have seemed like a princely sum. The man hired on, accompanying Ray to cattle auctions where he wrote huge checks he knew there was no money to cover . . .

Ray cornered him with the .22 cal. Jimmie begged for his life. Ray spared him for some strange reason. Really, considering what transpired later, Ray would have been much, much better off had he decided to silence him.

J. McCormick's story was more than enough "probable cause" to go digging around Copeland's farm. He swore they'd never find anything—and he wasn't lying; at least, not this time.

They found some old dog bones.

However, Copeland had hired himself out on a farm near Ludlow. He had done some "odd jobs" there. Odd jobs, indeed.

Digging in the floor of an old barn, the shallow graves began to be unearthed. "What's done in the darkness, shall be brought to the light," the Bible and Johnny Cash says.

Three bodies were unearthed from the barn. Then a fourth. All proved to be vagrants once employed by Ray Copeland.

The owner of the farm couldn't believe it. "He was always such a hard-working guy. Real conscientious." He might have kicked some shit quizzically while rhapsodizing on the Ray Copeland work ethic.

Ray tried to make out an insanity defense. Failing that, he resigned himself to his fate, but not before delivering the rather anti-climatic statement, "Well them things just happen sometimes," when informed that the wife he often used as a punching bag was *also* being charged.

Faye quite predictably protested her innocence. The tell-tale ledger of death, written in her own handwriting seemed to bear "mute testimony to murder," (to borrow the tile of an old E. C. Comics story).

Faye and Ray were arrested, tried, convicted; became the oldest couple to ever be sentenced to death in Missouri, at ages seventy-six and sixty-nine, respectively. Upon sentencing, Faye burst into tears. Ray, cold and emotionless till the end, reflected, "Well, those things just happen sometimes."

Ray died in prison in 1993, aged seventy-eight. Faye, after having had her sentence commuted to life, due to mitigating circumstances, died of terminal illness in 1999, after being released to a private nursing home.

C'est la vie.

CHAPTER 10

Like a Rat in His Shack

The Eccentric Life and Unhappy Death of Killer Eugene Butler

In light of the preceding chapter, we should probably take a few minutes to consider the crimes of North Dakota's virtually unknown Eugene Butler.

Eugene, apparently, was always considered "eccentric"; a true misanthrope, he virtually lived in seclusion in his shack, occasionally hiring farm hands and transients to help with the chores.

(Since I have been unable to find much in the way of detail concerning this most singular case, you may, once again, forgive me a little literary indulgence in a recreation based on stark details and imaginative fancy.)

†

The tall, scarecrow-like man shuffled around the confines of his filthy shack. Outside, Dub was busy pulling up weeds. Hmm. He didn't quite like the look of that one. He had seemed okay, sure enough, when he had hired on; but it was turning out to be the same with him as it was with the others before. Man was lazy, indolent; that was all there was to it. Sure, he did the chores, here and there, and took care of what was asked of him, and he always had a toothless grin to give whenever Eugene popped his head out the door or came up to him while he was hoeing the turnips. But Eugene knew full well you could hide a thousand sins behind a smile like that, hide a lie behind a grin, so to speak. He started getting the unhappy feeling that Dub was planning on robbing him, and maybe taking off. Where to? Most likely Canada.

"Maybe he can go up to the Yukon and prospect for gold," Eugene Butler laughed to himself. He had just been reading an article about Alferd Packer, a man who had led a group of prospectors up into the mountains of the Colorado territory and got snowed in by a dreadful storm. Well, come thawing out time, the only one to emerge alive from that shack was . . . Alferd Packer.

Crazy sumbitch had killed and *eaten* his companions to survive.

Eugene shuddered. He didn't know how a man could rightly batten on the flesh of another man, even as a matter of survival. Just the mere thought of it made him feel queasy. He walked over to the window. The clouds were lowering in the sky. Pretty soon Dub would come in, dirty, sweaty, smelling of rangy outdoors work and chewing tobacco, and expect to be fed. Then he would repair to his place in the spare room and strum his old beat-up guitar until he passed out late in the evening. He'd probably imbibe a nip or two from the flask Eugene knew he kept secreted on his person, too.

Eugene Butler frowned. He didn't approve of alcohol intake, but he hadn't said anything to Dub about his drinking. He didn't want to drive away his hired hand. But, he also had had a sneaking suspicion steal over him the last couple of days, a sort of tickling at the back of his neck. *Was* Dub planning on robbing him? He wasn't sure. But, he also knew the big man could easily overpower him, if he took a notion to. Eugene had been going back and forth over whether or not he wanted to take the chance.

"Say, them beans is special, old hoss. You care if I go in for a second helping?"

Dub chewed reflectively, bean juice dotting his face, dribbling down his dirty, greasy chin, staining his beard. Eugene didn't have it in him to be disgusted by anything; he had more than his fair share of unsavory habits.

But, as the big, sloppy, dirty farm hand went in to ecstacies over his dinner, he went back behind the stove, his blood pulsing in his veins.

Back behind the stove is where he kept the sledge. It felt like it was calling his name. He grasped the handle. He could feel the power in the wood. It had a greasy, grey, snaky feeling to it, and it made him feel durned hard in his pants.

He kept up chattering, small talk; "Yessum, I season 'em just the way you like 'em Dub. Plenty of fat back and grease, a pinch of pepper, half an onion, and some cayenne. Cayenne, that's my secret. No, you go right ahead and keep on eating. I've already had my fill . . ."

Dub was oblivious to the fact that death hovered just above his shoulders. Eugene Butler heaved a gusty sigh, raised his arms above his head, brought the hammer down with killing force, with hard, brutal intensity.

Smack, crack. Thwump!

Dub fell over onto the table, leaking his red fluid out from between his ears. His beans went lickety plop all over the table, mixing in a thick, viscous pool with the blood of the dead man. Eugene fancied he could see thermal waves, or ectoplasm. Or?

He sighed, Lord, he had a mess to clean up. And it was already well past six. He'd have to eat first, he reckoned. Man had to have his strength.

†

He put Dub with the others. Down the trap door, crawling with the body parts in a burlap sack. Into the dusk and dirt below the house. It was already a well-stocked little boneyard down here. Dub hadn't been the first one he reckoned might cause him problems, take from him—*him*—a poor, defenseless old man living alone. Why, that sort of behavior smacked of cold-blooded hostility, he figured, meeting kindness with envy, greed, violence, and theft. Not good, he reckoned. Not good at all. My God, he asked himself, as he buried the pieces of Dub down there in the dark, with the rats and other vermin scurrying just out of sight, What is this world a-coming to?

The howls and imprecations of the damned filled his ears that year. It was 1906 before the state hauled him, kicking and screaming, but mostly clueless, to the state hospital . . .nice place in those days.

Decades later, an actress named Francis Farmer would write a tell-all biography about *her* stay in a psychiatric hospital in the 1940s. It made for sensational reading.

Francis was forced to eat her own shit. Francis was forced to walk around naked, eat out of a trough with leering, zombie-like loons in a basement holding cell; Francis was treated to cold baths, insulin injections, electroshock, ad infinitum. If any of it was true, then what is generally known about (*ahem*) "psychiatric care facilities" in the era before widespread reforms was confirmed. Iconic muckraker Geraldo Rivera would, decades after Francis' ordeal, take hidden cameras inside a state hospital where he would find a macabre scene: inmates, treated little better than animals, stewed in their own filth, in deplorable, inhumane conditions. This was in the middle seventies, and that place has long since been closed to its eternal howls and its swirling, black hole void of lingering miseries. (Assuming, of course, the decrepit structure still stands.)

We can glean that the conditions under which Mr. Eugene Butler lived and ultimately died were not overly pleasant or conducive to mental and emotional recovery.

His death came in 1909. Upon his death, his property (which must have stood vacant for some time, holding its dark secrets within while, outside, the wind howled and moaned . . . but I, perhaps, become too poetical!) was put up for sale. Or inspected. Perhaps several of the young men once employed by Eugene Butler were missed, their whereabouts unknown, their eventual fate a concern to whatever meager familial relations they happened to possess.

It was the examination of the cellar, beneath the trap door, wherein a skull was eventually unearthed. Some digging later revealed more human bones, and more. A miniature graveyard kept, like some macabre spider's web wherein the little husks of dead flies hang, grimly, after the dreadful arachnid repast, was made evident to the law enforcement officers.

What could have been his motive? Mere insanity seemed the most likely culprit, with Eugene Butler uncommonly concerned that his hired hands might rat him out to authorities over business improprieties.

A more likely scenario, modern crime writers feel, is that Eugene Butler suffered from agonized, slumbering homosexual tendencies—which, in his era, were not something to readily confess, even to a doctor or alienist. These deep, unresolved conflicts and urges festered within him, until, finally, they reared their head in an ugly display of savage revenge and inhuman butchery that created a forgotten little graveyard beneath the floorboards of an abandoned North Dakota home.

CHAPTER 11

His Strange Revenge

The Sordid Saga of Andrew Kehoe

I suppose since, just today, a demented young man sat in on a prayer meeting at an historic black church and gunned down *nine* parishioners (including a state senator), it might be prudent to write about the shocking, forgotten saga of farmer Andrew Kehoe. At the risk of sensationalizing the cruel revenge killing of children, I feel I must expose the evil, vicious side of man for all to see—render him naked, thrust him out into the light. Also, I must underscore the fact that such mass violent attacks, while seemingly endemic in the second decade of the twenty-first century, are, in point of *fact*, nothing new—although admittedly they seem to be happening with greater and greater frequency in recent years.

†

Andrew Kehoe was a thoroughgoing SOB.

It seems he had been so since birth. Maybe it is revealing to expose the fact that his hated stepmother, whom he was given to arguing with much, was suddenly consumed one fine day by a fiery explosion of oil—her stove erupted like a bomb. Puzzlingly, her quick-witted and malignant enemy of a stepson poured a bucket of water on her. Which only caused the oil-based flames to spread.

She later died of her injuries. We don't suppose young Andrew had many tears to shed.

He eventually studied electrical engineering at the University of Michigan, taking his degree and going back home to torture his long-suffering wife.

†

A Mr. Ellsworth, a witness to the Bath school massacre, gives a firsthand account. Out planting melons in a farmyard that was in close proximity to both the schoolhouse (he relates that his vision of this place was obscured by dense woods), and the Kehoe farm, he was alerted that grim day of May 18, 1927, by a terrific explosion, which he counted as coming from the Kehoe property; most specifically, his sheep barn.

It was not a few moments before he was joined by his wife. The wife had come pouring out of the house, her skirt in her hands, yelling that "the school has just exploded!" Both husband and wife stood for a moment in disbelief as a column of gray smoke and ash poured into the air. Then, panicked suddenly at the fate of their son (who, amazingly, survived), Mr. and Mrs. Ellsworth piled into their rickety truck. The scene Mr. Ellsworth recounts in his book, *The Bath School Disaster*, is breathtaking:

> We got to the school and as we ran across the lawn we met some people who told us our boy, who was in the second grade, was out and all right. I think there were about ten or a dozen people there at that time. The wall had crumbled each way, letting the edge of the roof drop on the brick and cement. There was a pile of children of about five or six under the roof and some of them had arms sticking out, some had legs, and some just their heads sticking out. They were unrecognizable because they were covered with dust, plaster, and blood. There were not enough of us to move the roof. It looked as if hardly anything held it at the top.

The scene of carnage was something most had never before witnessed. Ellsworth, telling the men he is going for rope by which to try and pull the fallen roof off the survivors, jumps back into his truck. Rumbling along, he passes Andrew Kehoe, who gives a devilish grin of "both rows of his teeth . . . I can see them now!" Ellsworth makes special note of this, the crazed, menacing toothsome grin of Andrew Kehoe etched indelibly in his subconscious.

Others witnessed the madcap apparition of the insane bomber; local farmers, a member of the school board and his son; both of whom, Ellsworth recounts, Mr. Kehoe had had some small "trouble" with from time to time. (His last check to Warden Keys he dropped, saying, "My boy, you want to take good care of that check as it is probably the last check you will ever get.") Ellsworth speculated, almost assuredly correctly, that if Kehoe had run into them, he would certainly have shot them both that day.

Of course, the *next* (and as it turned out, final) act in the mad horror story of the Bath School Disaster was coming. Crazed terroristic murderer Andrew Kehoe sat (I presume) along Main Street, and, igniting an incendiary device, blew *himself* to kingdom come, igniting the tops of nearby cars, sending glass and debris and wreckage flying in a deadly, missile-like wave.

The resultant victims, according to Ellsworth, were "unrecognizable." A Mr. Huyck lay in the center of the street, his leg missing, imploring the first responders, to "Leave me, boys! The trees are full of it!" (He assumed, incorrectly, but understandably, that they were under some sort of enemy attack.) Other bodies were mutilated and shredded beyond repair.

The tops of cars were ablaze, but those fires it is said were easily extinguished. A man ran forward with a belt to staunch the massive flow of blood from Huyck's leg . . . but, he died anyway. With his wife at his side. Or, so it is written.

Ambulances pulled up. The effort to free victims at the school seemed to involve the use of a telephone pole as a sort of lever.

Local doctors and a pharmacist, Mr. Crum, arrived on the scene shortly after, Mr. Crum and his wife converting their pharmacy into a makeshift clinic to treat the wounded. Firemen and state troopers arrived, going into the basement of the school, where, so Mr. Ellsworth claims, *500* pounds of TNT were recovered, the clocks and detonators clipped in the nick of time, it would seem. (When asked later why they braved such a deadly task, the heroic men solemnly proclaimed, "It is our duty.")

Children were brought out bloodied, covered in plaster and debris; some missing limbs, all mutilated by the blast. One woman sat, it is written, with a dead little girl on each side of her, in the grass, trying in vain to cope with the full scope of the monstrous horror that had just unfolded. In front of her, her little son lay dying. She lost him.

(One finds that particular image hard to let go of.)

Of course, the makeshift morgue, set up in City Hall, was a busy place. Families used their personal vehicles to shuttle the little dead to their respective undertaking parlors. It was grim, grim work.

The following Sunday saw a reported multitude turn out to visit at various memorials and funerals, an overwhelming show of sympathy that touched Mr. Ellsworth, as reported thousands poured out to pay their respects to the stricken town. Predictable mourning and chest-thumping resounded, and the morbid, morose beat went on and on. Mr. Ellsworth takes time to examine, in his book, the one question that was on everyone's mind: What on Earth or in the darkest pits of Hell could possess a man to do such a cowardly, murderous, and downright despicable and, yes, evil act? It is a question we are asking to this very day, time and again.

"The Worst Demon Ever!"

Mr. Ellsworth so names Mr. Kehoe in the opening salvo of the chapter examining his life. Mr. Kehoe, as has already been mentioned, was a thoroughgoing SOB of a variety and type that was not rare in those days when Horatio Alger not infrequently bore vampire fangs in his honest, all-American face. One sees a picture of Andrew Kehoe, rearing back at a desk, in a reclining position, as if he had all the world at his hard-fisted beck-and-call . . . it is a pose both arrogant and baffling, something worthy of an Andrew Carnegie. Andrew Kehoe, however, was no self-made billionaire or magnate. We can only speculate as to what demons saddled his back through the days of his short, unhappy life.

(Was it really short and unhappy? One imagines that same befuddling, arrogant grin pasted across his face as he blew himself up in his car, the explosive fire ripping through his cheeks and jowls and stifling the final, bloodcurdling laugh as it came screeching out of his mouth. It was swallowed by the volcanic rumble of the all-consuming gasoline fire; but, really, one imagines if Kehoe screamed, it was with peals of mirth. After all, he was going out with the proverbial "bang." Wink, wink.)

The portrait drawn of Kehoe has, as its centerpiece, the probable murder of his stepmother. Whom, incidentally, but not surprisingly, he hated.

One imagines the stiff, ugly Victorian dame coming home from her day to town, turning on the oil stove . . . and having it explode all over her. The unfortunate woman bursting into flames, writhing in agony as young Andrew stands there. His hand over his mouth. What is he to do? He takes a bucket to douse her with water, of course only spreading the oily fire further. The woman, having missed the Dick Van Dyke Saturday morning commercials about "Stop, drop, and roll Dick roll!" did none of this, ran outside in agony, and finally died of the unfortunate "happenstance." Neighbors, knowing the young boy's predilection for tinkering, suspected that budding psychopath Andrew must have had *something* to do with that stove mysteriously, inexplicably exploding. (Alternately, perhaps, they put it down to an "Act of God." Either way, no charges were ever brought against anyone, and the poor woman was consigned to her cold, unlucky grave.)

Andrew is described as a tinkerer, a Catholic (he helped build the church and then refused to pay the builders after being assessed $400. When the local priest came calling, demanding the money, Andrew Kehoe told him, in no uncertain terms, he was to take a hike; or, alternately, he would be kicked out on his ass. Which must have ended the Kehoes' involvement with Masses on Sunday, at midnight, or any other damn time of the day or week.)

Likewise, Andrew showed the same solitary, bitter, "never give an inch," mentality in *all* his dealings with others. Though his wife, Nellie, was, albeit, described as "lovely," Andrew himself is described as not being happy unless he was tinkering with machinery, electrical wires, gadgetry, etc. Mr. Ellsworth, weirdly, gives the "Worst Demon" credit for being very progressive in his farming methods, in always looking for new and innovative ways to do common chores.

Mr. Kehoe had inherited the family farm in Bath Township from his good-natured doctor father. Andrew himself did not care for farming, let the place go run-to-riot, and worked his animals like . . . animals. (Cruelly harsh, I take it. He must have had a barnyard of lean nags and starving cows, mangy chickens losing their feathers—that sort of thing.) Stench and filth abounding, perhaps, while the strange "Lord of the Manor," who, at this point, had become distant and increasingly hostile and paranoid, was tinkering in his machine shop, only at peace when immersed in gears and wires and cogs, fingers dripping with oil.

(Note: Actually, Mr. Ellsworth makes a point of the fact that the left-brained Kehoe was actually very fastidious about his appearance, having always made sure to spruce up before he was seen out on the street. I suppose vanity and narcissistic psychosis walk hand-in-hand in some men.)

Other notable instances of Kehoe's soft, sugary, thoroughly-humanitarian ethics include shooting the neighbor's puppy and beating one of his horses to death for refusing to pull a manure cart. Mr. Ellsworth gives us the image of the unfortunate dray's corpse being carted away to a rendering plant, no doubt to be turned into glue.

But Monty Ellsworth did seem to like Andrew Kehoe; before, of course, Mr. Kehoe detonated a bomb in a school killing thirty-two town children. Mr. Kehoe, the notable mechanical genius, helped the gas station owner install pipes. They likewise went shooting together, and Mr. Ellsworth gives a long digressive exposition of this, culminating in the observation that Andrew Kehoe showed "not the slightest nervousness," despite the horrific finality of the homicidal and suicidal action he was about to undertake.

Mr. Kehoe was known previously to have purchased a large quantity of dynamite. Not unusual for a farmer in those days, although, today, the ATF, FBI, NSA, and Homeland Security would definitely be alerted by such a purchase. After all, it was (as mentioned earlier) *500* pounds of explosive material. What on earth could Mr. Kehoe want with such a large amount?

"I aim to sell to local farmers who might need a supply," he claimed.

Sure.

†

Motive, motive, motive . . .

On the Monday before he killed the schoolchildren, Mr. Kehoe most likely murdered his wife. Her body was found buried in a hog pen a mere day after the tragedy. Thousands had traipsed through the place to see the remains of the exploded farmhouse, none of them suspecting that Mrs. Kehoe was buried literally beneath their feet.

Motive, motive, motive . . .

It appears, according to (*ahem*) an "online resource" that Mrs. Andrew Kehoe was indeed suffering from the then almost universally fatal affliction of tuberculosis . . .which, unbelievably , killed quite a few people in the era before antibiotics. (Silent screen stars such as Mabel Normand and Lucille Ricksen both died from TB in the late twenties/early thirties.) Tuberculosis wards were filled with those choking out the last minutes of their lives with the deadly disease, and Mrs. Kehoe, being no exception, must have found it increasingly unbearable to deal both with her increasing physical deterioration and her increasingly psychotic husband. Some folks are just born to such happy fates.

It is likewise suggested that the bank was going to *foreclose* on the Kehoe house and farm property, and that Mr. Kehoe had consistently failed to meet his mortgage payments for, oh, months and months and months. Probably true. What could be a more fitting motive for wiring the whole damnable place up with a makeshift electrical apparatus and make it go *kablooey* than the idea that some double-breasted, suit-wearing banker is going to get his greedy mitts on what you have worked so hard and so long to attain? What else? A man like Mr. Kehoe might find satisfaction in sending the whole kit-and-kaboodle sky high, floating on fiery clouds to some burnt ash and cinder afterlife, as a final, parting "fuck you!" to polite, workaday, American tea-sipper society? What? I ask you!

Monty Ellsworth begins his book by laying out the tax situation as per re: the Bath School, which his friend Mr. Kehoe massacred. Taxes, apparently, were high, so that as appointed treasurer Kehoe often argued that taxes . . . should not be so high.

Tax details are a serious yawn, but to Mr. Kehoe, who argued that taxes should be lowered, they were most decidedly *not* a yawn. Thus, the Great American Psychotic Bulldog barked and snarled and shook his jowls, and found himself butting heads with the other members of the school board, all of whom we're imagining as a tight-fisted, bloodless lot with pale complexions, watering eyes, thin, withered lips, long noses that icicles might form at the tip of, and especially, creepy, long, skinny fingers. Also, almost universally bald.

The phlegmatic Kehoe was a far cry from that lot, I imagine, (he actually bears a striking resemblance, in one photograph I have seen of him reclining in his chair with a cigar, to Leonardo Dicaprio. An actor, by the way, who cannot be accused of having aged well , I think) and so their personal or professional or whatever scorn of him cut down to the bone, in a place where his pride and ego and smoldering homicidal rage all lived like veritable brothers. He was eventually voted off the school board, much to his . . . well, we can assume, based on his actions later, that it didn't make him happy.

For his malicious drubbing at the hands of his fellow school board members, he blamed a *Mr. Huyck* . . . his nemesis. The "Bad Guy". The "*persecutor*" in the mind of the so-rapidly becoming unhinged former Bath School Treasurer.

Mr. Ellsworth noted, as stated before, that, if Kehoe had managed to run into Huyck and his son downtown on the day of the fatal blast, he would have promptly shot both of them. As it was, Huyck died as a bystander during the last blast of the day—the suicide of *his* personal nemesis—Mr. Andrew Kehoe.

But what about those forty-odd bodies? Why kill all the children? Was Mr. Kehoe that much of a vindictive sonofabitch, to not only go to his own death (we assume with that same shit-eating grin plastered all over his face) but to also take a chain-gang of little souls into the afterlife with him?

Apparently so.

Monty Ellsworth wrote that he felt Kehoe was brooding for a month beforehand, planning and plotting his strange revenge accordingly. When it hit the proverbial fan, he had invoked a "scorched earth" policy that might have made Der Fuhrer proud seventeen, eighteen years later. He had even thought of wiring his horse's feet together, so they couldn't run away from the blast, so they would be destroyed, too.

Five hundred pounds of TNT hidden in the south wing of the school basement, and if his *second* detonator device had gone off, the whole thing could have been much, much worse. As it was, little children were blown to kingdom come, dying in a fiery inferno, screaming and crying in a white hot moment of agony, never knowing why Hell had hit them so suddenly, so strikingly from out of the morning blue.

Outside, running around downtown Bath, a madman in a rickety truck perambulated about with a ghoulish grin, a chortle or guffaw of sick exultation escaping from his lungs a bare moment before he blasted himself to the fiery gates of Hell . . . and took innocent bystanders, those unlucky enough to be caught in the maelstrom of the explosive charge, with him.

(Mr. Ellsworth, by the way, appraises us of the device used to set *all* the buildings of the Kehoe property alight, being a full bottle of kerosene in a chicken coop, wired to a timepiece with a sparkplug. This in turn connected with wires to all the other buildings, snaking through the yard like the hot wires of insanity in their creator's head.)

An act of cowardly terrorism, to be sure. One that, today, is almost forgotten. Forty souls, most of them children, met their fiery fate that May day of 1927. Chained to the memory of their killer, we can still see him blowing himself up in that rickety Ford pickup, the cartoonish, psychopathic grin, the blood and fire in his teeth, his burning eyes . . . I am being, if you'll forgive me, a tad melodramatic.

Andrew Kehoe is buried in an unmarked grave. No wonder. It's a stark little plot in a lonely, desolate boneyard.

And, really, that's all I can stand to write on the subject of Andrew Kehoe.

CHAPTER 12

The Closing-Time Killer

Richard Carpenter

The punk walked into the bar, a crooked grin cracking his skinny, ugly visage.

The bartender, a large, affable man with a world-weary grin, said, "Hey buddy, you're in luck. I'm just about to close, but I got time for one more. You can have a drink."

The bartender started to ask the punk what he wanted, but his voice died in his throat. The punk pulled out twin pistols, aimed them like he thought this was Dodge City and he was Bat fucking Masterson.

"The money. How about the money?"

There was one other patron in the bar, an off-duty cop. He quickly went for his gun, but the punk spat out, in movie tough-guy fashion, "You better put that gat away, or someone will die here tonight!"

Officer Bosacki did as he was told. The bartender, who professed to not wanting any trouble, gave the punk the money. The punk, a psychotic mama's boy named Richard Carpenter, for his part was most pleased, but instructed plainly, "Hand it all over, and don't bother with the silver—just the green stuff." Or, something to that effect.

After collecting what he wanted (including Officer Medard Bosacki's gun), the punk bolted. Bosacki and the barkeep chased the kid out into the streets, but he vanished as if the night was his personal cloak.

"The kid disappeared faster than anyone I've ever seen."

So we begin the loser saga of Richard Carpenter, a devoted son and loving brother, as well as a cold-blooded armed robber and cop killer.

Carpenter committed a string of robberies—around seventy by 1955—and was known as a "cool customer, an intelligent criminal," who would reason with his victims, telling them, "Just stay calm. See how calm I am? Just cooperate and nothing bad will happen to you. But, if you give me any trouble, you'll get it in the guts." (Again, words to that effect.)

Police estimated Carpenter had made around *fourteen grand* from his total robberies; not bad for someone who stuck, primarily, to gas station heists and sticking up seedy bars and liquor stores. They also figured that, eventually, owing to the way he swung his revolvers around in such a cavalier fashion, he was going to end up snuffing some innocent person. They felt it was inevitable.

And they weren't remiss in thinking this.

†

The heat was closing in on him, but Carpenter knew he had a lucky streak a mile wide. He was lying low in a movie theater, sleeping in the back row, when an off-duty cop recognized him.

The cop approached warily, knowing already what a tough customer Carpenter was. He went up to the kid, nudged him, said, "Hey, hey buddy, why are you sleeping in here?"

Richard might have peeped one eye open, said something smart. We don't know. We do know that Carpenter told him it was none of his business, that he had just come inside to "cool off."

"I'm a police officer. You better come with me."

The cop—Kerr—led Carpenter out of the theater, but the punk stumbled on the walk outside. This threw Kerr off balance, and gave Carpenter an opportunity to come up with his gun. He fired a shot at Kerr's chest, and the officer returned fire, striking Carpenter in the leg.

Wounded leg or not, the punk took off, leaving Kerr on the sidewalk. As his hysterical wife (who had accompanied him to the theater that night) approached him, he began to complain bitterly that, "It was Carpenter! It was him! I know it!"

Indeed.

Officer Kerr survived, if only by a hair's breadth; another officer that had had the misfortune to encounter Carpenter earlier had not been so lucky. Officer Murphy had apprehended the shabby Carpenter on the subway. Promptly arresting him, he led the punk out of the subway station and into the street. There he made a fatal mistake.

He stopped to make sure of the identity of the suspect. As his attention was diverted for a split second, Carpenter had time to draw a concealed firearm. He shot Officer Murphy in the chest, killing him instantly. Also, sealing his own fate.

†

Injured, the savage little reprobate ran to a residential neighborhood, found himself at the back door of the home of truck driver Leonard Powell.

Mr. Powell opened the back door to a small, scruffy, bleeding kid pointing two revolvers at him.

"I guess you know who I am," said Richard.

"I guess I do," answered Mr. Powell.

"Hey, you better let me in. If you and your family do what I say, I won't harm you. I promise. But if you do anything against me, I'll kill you."

Mrs. Powell came to the back door. Mr. Powell calmly told her, "Darling, this is Richard Carpenter. He says that if we do what he says, he won't harm us. Don't scream."

Mrs. Powell managed to maintain her composure.

"Well, you'd better not let Bobby (her son, who was in the living room watching the reports of the manhunt for Richard on the news) see that gun!"

So for a day and a half, Richard Carpenter was holed up in the Powell home, holding them hostage, watching the news coverage of himself with some obvious amusement.

(Note: It should be stated that Richard, unlike many a criminal, reportedly had no vices: didn't drink, smoke, visit prostitutes, and was even known, as a cabbie, to refuse fares to known houses of "ill-repute." He was likewise a loner, with no friends. What his ultimate motive for a sudden crime spree could possibly be, beyond an innate sense of narcissism, can only be conjectured at.)

The news coverage detailed Richard's sorry life, from broken home, to devotion to his sainted mother, sisters, and grandfather (of whom he claimed he was careful to always bring "three good cigars a day").

Richard, wounded, and by this time probably thoroughly exhausted, began to ramble.

"You all can't think very much of me . . . but I don't care anything about it anyway," he told the Powells. "It's been a lousy life, but if I had one regret, it's that I never did anything to make my mother and my sisters proud."

Mr. Powell, sensing their captor was on the verge of psychological meltdown, said, "Well, I think you could be a very good person. I'm sorry you find yourself in such a mess."

This sympathy ploy worked, and Richard, clearly not thinking ahead too many steps, decided to let the whole family go outside for some air.

The whole family did. And they quickly made their escape, running to the houses of neighbors and warning them that there was a gunman loose, and that they needed to contact law enforcement immediately.

Richard, who was soon surrounded by a veritable policeman's convention of law enforcement personnel, decided that it would be meet and good not to surrender, but fire a volley at the overwhelming force arrayed against him.

The cops returned fire, shattering the glass as Carpenter moved past the window. He was not through yet, though.

He climbed from a window, out onto the roof of the building, jumping, despite his injured leg, to another roof. There he climbed down into another apartment, and fired again.

He was met with a return volley. The cops charged the building, finding a cowering young man inside, a young man who claimed, "It's not me you want! I live here!"

"It's *you,* Carpenter!" answered the arresting officer.

Carpenter died in the electric chair at Joliet, March 16, 1956. The only other thing I can say about him, is that, in the one photograph I've seen of him, he bears an uncanny resemblance to the popular actor Christian Bale.

CHAPTER 13

The Ypsilanti Woman Slayer

John Norman Collins

Before Ted Bundy, the most famous co-ed slayer in American history was John Norman Collins.

Two young boys discover a body on an abandoned farm. What specifically they were doing out there was anyone's guess. The remains are of a young woman named Mary Fleszar, apprehended and murdered by an unknown assailant July 9, 1967, while walking back to her apartment in Ypsilanti, Michigan. Mary is a college co-ed.

The last person to see her alive is a neighbor, who describes a dark grey Chevrolet truck driven by an unidentified suspect. The truck pulled up alongside Mary Fleszar. The perception of the witness was that the unidentified perpetrator was attempting to pick Mary up. Mary shook her head twice, walking quickly away. She was never seen again.

Questions . . .

A young man, unidentified except as a "dark haired, good-looking, young, white man," enters the funeral home wherein the body of the unfortunate Mary Fleszar is currently stored. He asks to see the body, claims he is a "friend of the family," wants to get one final picture with . . . the body. He is rebuffed by the staff of the funeral parlor, who, under the circumstances, said that the young man's request would "just not be in keeping with standard operating procedures."

But, for some reason, these mortuary workers cannot give an adequate description of this young man.

(It is a matter of general knowledge that psychotic killers, of the sexual variety, as exemplified by the Ypsilanti Woman Slayer, like to keep trophies to gloat over, and relive the thrill later: These can be panties, locks of hair, a human ear or finger, or photographs.)

The Psychic and the Psycho

Peter Hurkos was a world-renowned "psychic" (if you believe in that sort of thing), who was often, during the sixties and seventies, brought in on criminal cases to help intuitively sniff out missing children or find the culprit behind certain crimes. He was featured on such classic television programs as *In Search Of* and *One Step Beyond* (who did an entire dramatization based on the Peter Hurkos story). Mr. Hurkos first learned of his extraordinary abilities during the war, when, as an operative for the Dutch resistance, he fell from a ladder while fleeing the Nazis.

Later, while convalescing with his ostensible comrades, they begin to suspect him of being a spy or double agent. Deciding quite quickly, under the circumstances, to put a pillow over his head to smother him to death, his comrades commence to commit his murder. In a panic, he begins a series of psychic predictions that convince them to do otherwise; that prove to them, in effect, that the information he has is genuinely gained through paranormal sources, and not gleaned from being a double crosser or Nazi collaborator.

Thus, his latent ESP ability, brought to the forefront perhaps because of his fall, actually saved his life. (Or so it is claimed.)

The preceding narrative was dramatized quite successfully on the cult fifties paranormal anthology program *One Step Beyond*. The real Hurkos became a celebrity psychic in the same manner in which Uri Geller did perhaps a decade later, crisscrossing Europe and America and appearing on television and film, before finally being brought in by police departments as a special aid to stalled investigations. More on that in a moment.

July 1, 1968, was the preceding of an angry, revolutionary period. Civil Rights, anti-Vietnam War agitation, student rebellions of every stripe . . . moon landings, Rock 'N' Roll, dope, Free Love and *Dark Shadows*, baby. You rather get the tie-dyed point, I take it.

Smile on your brother . . .

At any rate, one man who was certainly *not* smiling on his brother was the Ypsilanti Co-Ed Killer, who abducted, raped, beat mercilessly, and then summarily snuffed the life from student Joan Schell, who was stabbed forty-seven times. Her body was discovered in Ann Arbor, July 9 of '68, and the Ypsilanti sex killer was just getting warmed up.

(Collins was questioned about Schell early on, as he was *the last seen with her*—but he was described as a "personable" young man, and the cops bought his story. A charming psychopath, in other words.)

In quick succession followed:

Jane Mixer—shot and strangled, dumped in a cemetery. Eight months had elapsed, and the score, so far, was cops– 0, killer–3.

March 25, 1969, the body of Maralynn Skelton, who had been hitchhiking near a shopping center when she met her untimely fate. Known as a wild girl, a "party girl," she was renowned for running with the proverbial "bad crowd." It was March 24 when the sixteen-year-old was last seen alive; her body was found a day later, near Earhart Road and Glacier Way in Ypsilanti. The killer had apparently worked out a savage, brutal way of working out his own sexual frustrations upon the body of Maralynn, who had been beaten remorselessly with a belt, raped, and then strangled with a garter. Again, no suspects, no trail of evidence.

The killer next picked a literal child to victimize. Thirteen-year-old Dawn Basom was abducted on April 15 of that year; she was last seen leaving a dormitory on the EMU campus. The youngest of the victims, she had been strangled with a piece of electrical cord, and then unceremoniously dumped later; although it was supposed she might have been abused and killed in a nearby barn, where much of her clothing was found.

Alice Kalom was a University of Michigan graduate, last seen at the Depot House in Ann Arbor dancing with a young man "with long hair." Her body was found near US 23; she had been raped, shot, and stabbed twice in the chest. She was twenty-three, her clothing was scattered about, perhaps for ritualistic reasons; and, curiously, her shoes were missing.

Karen Sue Beineman, eighteen, was a freshman at East Michigan U when she disappeared after accepting a ride on a motorcycle from a stranger. Perhaps she thought he was tall, dark, and handsome. Certainly, he dispossessed her of any romantic notions about himself quite quickly. He strangled her, dumped her body in a ravine off of Huron Drive. Ironically, she had just left her parents a note assuring them of how "careful" she was being. The killer had beaten her mercilessly in the face, perhaps rendering it mostly unrecognizable.

Roxie Phillips' story is more unusual.

Hailing from Salinas, California, her body was found dumped in Pescadero Canyon near Carmel, California—strangled, raped, with personal possessions strewn about in the same ritualistic manner.

A friend proclaimed that a smooth, good-looking white man calling himself "John" had pulled up on a motorcycle a few days earlier, a guy with dark hair.

She met this guy while he was cruising near Roxie Phillips's residence. Michigan and California, of course, are geographically quite separate places; *but*, it turns out Mr. Collins *was* visiting the state at precisely that time, for medical treatment. Go figure.

(California, it was once remarked, might be termed by some as the "serial killer state," as so many of them seem to hail from that particular left coast, still-Wild West land of luxury and vice. Now, there is something to put on a travel brochure: "California! Come Visit the 'Serial Killer' State!")

Another possible victim, a tragic thirteen-year-old named Eileen Adams, had a nail hammered into her skull when her body was found: beaten, raped, and strangled, she was arranged suggestively with her stockings pulled up, after being abducted from her Ohio home. The body was found just outside of Ypsilanti, of course; the weapon of dispatch had been a black electrical cord, and there was the same characteristic beating of the face.

Incidentally, the presumably little body had been stuffed into an old sack.

†

So far, the police had no clues, but they *did* have six corpses, all of which had been found in rural areas between Ann Arbor and Ypsilanti. The location of the bodies formed a tight ring of sites, and the victims, more often than not, had been students or graduates of the EMU. The police, of course, were now looking for a campus prowler.

An abandoned farmhouse they felt, and a root cellar, were probably locations for these heinous torture-murders to take place. All of the victims had been deposited in areas where they would be easily discovered, the "lovers' lane"-type spots where young people go to neck. The man quite obviously was mobile, and was charming enough, it seemed, to coax victims into his car.

The women bore striking similarities in color of hair, appearance, etc., suggesting that the killer definitely preferred a type.

†

The young girl paused a moment on the shoulder of the road.

Should she? She needed a ride, but the idea of getting into a car with three strange guys was a little daunting. What if they were rapists or something? Suddenly, she wanted to walk away, to get out of there. But one of the guys leaned out the window, his arm resting on the door, and said, "Hey, honey, you want a ride or not?"

He was wearing an EMU sweater, was big, good looking. Suddenly, against her better judgment, she found herself sliding into the back seat. Making herself comfortable, despite how nervous she felt.

She decided that it was probably all right, though. These guys looked like the sort of jockey, "boy next door" types she had grown up with. Weren't they EMU students?

"Hi. I'm John . . ." said one of the guys. He held out his hand, which was big and powerful-looking, and broad like a dinner plate.

"Hi, I'm Joan, Nice to meet you. She put out her hand, grasping his. He took it firmly but gently; his hands were rough, calloused she noted.

They were also icy cold.

And that was the final ride of Joan Schell.

†

Joan Schell lived a few blocks from victim Mary Fleszar. Her boyfriend, AWOL from the Army, was the first and most logical suspect.

A polygraph cleared the errant young buck private of any wrongdoing—at least, insomuch as the brutal murder of his former girlfriend was concerned.

Witnesses whispered that Joan Schell had been seen in the company of John Collins, a tall, dark-haired, attractive brute of a man living across the street. The police, as heretofore mentioned, interviewed Mr. Collins, who was so charming and personable that he completely snowed the detectives, capping his interview with a jaunty, "I sure hope you catch that guy!"

(If you wonder at the seeming naïvety of the cops, simply keep in mind that Collins, and most every other narcissistic psychopath, is able to put up a convincing front, screen, or "mask"; all the better to fool and beguile potential victims and the unwary. And also, who would suspect a teaching student of such a heinous crime, after all?)

I can take the time here to mention the first instance of a famous psychic being connected with this case. Jeanne Dixon. The world-renowned seeress who is said to have correctly predicted the assassination of President John F. Kennedy, was rumored, by increasingly uneasy students of EMU, to have predicted a "mass murder wave" around the Ann Arbor area, affecting a number of colleges . . . Dixon, for her part, denied ever making such a claim. Perhaps she should have taken credit, anyway.

Meanwhile, the bodies were piling up, having met their deaths in ever more violent ways. Nails hammered into heads, electrical cord and stockings wrapped around the throats . . . the killer leaving items behind at the scene of each grisly murder, ritualistic items meant to taunt the police. Who was this man?

Enter, finally, Peter Hurkos.

Hurkos, whose career at this point was heavily flagging due to his total "misses" while involved in the Boston Strangler Case, was offered by a local group calling itself the "Psychedelic Rangers," an exorbitant amount of money to come and assist in finding the Ypsilanti Woman Slayer. Hurkos at first declined, as the $25,000 he *wanted* was not forthcoming. Instead, a paltry grand was put up by the erstwhile "Rangers"—hardly a temptation for a night club attraction like Hurkos.

However, the "Psychic Detective" found his career in a bit of a puddle. So, he packed his bags, flew out from LA to the frosty wilds of Michigan, and, making himself an unwanted thorn in the bosom of local law enforcement, asked to see and handle evidence. A matter the local sheriff took a dim view towards.

Hurkos was ensconced in a hotel room that July of 1969. It was only a short time later that a mysterious young man arrived at the hotel, bearing a grim message for the renowned clairvoyant. The message intimated where the site of another body would be found, but the man who delivered the message, at this point, was most certainly *not* to be found. Excited, Hurkos summoned law enforcement to the spot but finally figured out, after an additional phone call (one threatening that, if Hurkos didn't *amscray*, *he* would be personally responsible for the next murder), that the killer was simply taunting him. The police remained unamused.

How much more unamused could they have been at the wildly flailing "descriptions" of the killer-at-large—all delivered by Hurkos with an assurance that he was "hot," and on the right trail.

The killer was described as blonde, "baby-faced," twenty-five to twenty-six years of age, and a motorcycle rider. Hurkos elaborated, puzzlingly naming the man as a "sick homosexual," and a member of some sort of fetishistic, Satanic cult that was into blood drinking. (One imagines, if it had been twenty years later, iconic television talk show pioneer Geraldo Rivera would have had a veritable orgiastic *field day* sticking his nose, microphone, and camera into the sordid, bloody mess of the Ypsilanti Co-Ed Slayings. But I digress.)

Taking to the airwaves less than a week after his arrival, Hurkos assured a frightened, desperate viewership that the "battle between Good and Evil," was one he intended to win. He also predicted that the body count would go as high as *nineteen*.

Note: Not to seem as if we are bashing this man entirely (after all, don't speak ill of the dead, even if they are fair game as far as libel laws are concerned), Hurkos by this point had changed his earlier wildly-inaccurate prediction to a much more reasonable, "The killer is six foot tall, has brown (dark?) hair." Maybe he just needed a few days to warm up.

Hurkos left within the week, after having gone to various crime scenes, while the local sheriff rolled his eyes, scowled, walked around with his hands on his hips, and most probably blew air through heavy, puffy jowls.

Like McArthur, he vowed to return soon and continue the fight. Traditional police work, and a little luck, beat him to the punch, however.

The Arrest

The Sheriff's special task force had tried creative methods to lay their hands on the man. One leaves a particularly jarring image in our mind, for some reason.

After one of the bodies had been removed from the crime scene, it was replaced with a department store mannequin, in the hopes that a stakeout would apprehend the killer. Since many of these men are known to have ritualistic peccadillos, it was assumed he might return to the scene. After all, the body of Fleszar, the first victim, had been hidden, presumably for a month, before the killer had moved it to a spot where it could be more conveniently happened upon.

(I wonder, myself, at the artifice involved in replacing the body with a mannequin. Was it positioned correctly? How far did the police department go toward verisimilitude? Am I seriously wondering at the aesthetics of this macabre footnote?)

In what could only be a scene culled from a cheap movie, a "jogger" happened by, and a policeman failed in his attempt to radio in a report. Due to technical problems?

The rain was pouring. The cop, we must assume, made a vain attempt to follow the mysterious, suspect, crime-scene jogger who decided to visit in the pouring rain—only to hear a car door slam, an engine rev, and a motorist hightail it out of the area. Close, but no banana.

Detectives had already questioned one young man, *John Norman Collins*, as a suspect, but had earlier dismissed him. Now, they were not so sure. After talking to the girls at the wig shop where the last victim had last been seen getting on to a motorbike with a stranger, and making a composite that resembled Collins's mug eerily, they talked to former girlfriends, who verified that Mr. Collins drove a Triumph motorbike. Moreover, a relative who worked for the police department, when informed that Mr. Collins was a chief suspect, felt "incredulous," but nonetheless, remembering a stain he had found on the basement floor when Collins had been down there doing some "work," went to scrape up fragments of it. This turned out to be merely varnish, but the scent was baited; for Collins, the trap was sprung, the jig was up.

He tearfully protested his innocence while on the phone to his relative, the one whose basement he had used to cut the hair of the little boy. The place was ransacked; finally, hair samples and cloth fragments matching those belonging to one of the victims was unearthed. It appeared that Collins was *The Man*.

The ensuing trial revolved around the eyewitness identification of Collins as the man with the Triumph motorbike. (Friends privately confessed that Collins was so criminally reprobate he refused to spend money maintenancing the bike, and simply stole and burglarized parts for it.) Also, the infant science of forensics was still formidable enough to tie the hair samples and cloth fragments found buried in the basement to the murdered women . . .Collins was still denying his culpability decades later, after escape attempts and what must have, before long, been a personal realization that society would never see him as a free man, ever again.

As to what drove the psychopathic monster to act out in such a heinous disregard for life, we are given to understand he had a smothering, bizarrely enmeshed relationship with his mother, a la Norman Bates.

Two Normans. But Tony Perkins was far more handsome, don't you agree?

CHAPTER 14

Gunning for Babyface

Lester Gillis

(Alias: George Nelson)

The psychotic little bastard started across the hot highway, his gun blazing. Planted deep within the ditch at the side of the road, the two officers kept shooting . . . and shooting . . . and shooting.

Blood poured out from the little man, spattering in his teeth, in his eyes. His vision was a blur of sweat and heat and gore and anger. His very glance could probably have dropped birds from the sky dead.

He took round after round in his little, compact body, but he kept coming. It must have been sheer hate that drove him on, sheer evil that kept the body moving across that blacktop, into the gunfire, into the mouth of Hell.

Finally, because even the power of his indomitable will was not enough to sustain him the hail of gunfire that pierced his body, he fell; gave up the ghost. Died under the yawning gaze of a God that must have damned him.

His name was Lester Gillis. Or George Nelson. The world, though, knew him better as "Babyface." His story begins on the mean streets of Chicago, in an era long, long gone.

†

He grew up tough, did Lester Gillis. It was his small stature (this author, also being rather short, can attest to the fact that such disadvantages can weigh heavily on the psyches of developing males). The other kids tended to bully him, pick on him; girls snubbed him. Inside, he grew hard, feisty, even hostile. It wasn't something that happened all at once; like a wall, it was built, brick by painful brick.

Young Lester George Gillis Nelson (whatever), took to crime like the proverbial fish takes to icy drink: with a dogged, determined vengeance born out of his dire hatred for established society and everything it represented. Born next to the stinking, offal-strewn Chicago stockyards, he was curiously accustomed to the odor of Hell from his tenderest years.

(His tenderest years were spent, incidentally, in and out of reform school. His earliest bit of malfeasance involved shooting a young schoolyard chum in the jaw. *Aw,* the bygone days of innocent youth!)

It has been variously reported that he worked for the Touhey Mob, or Capone. Whatever the case, Gillis graduated from the petty gangsterism of stripping tires off automobiles (with the so-creatively named tire heist gang, "The Strippers"), to the more egregious crimes of a shake-down man in local whorehouses. Even at the young age of sixteen or so, Gillis/Nelson was plumbing the sordid depths of the social milieu.

He would waltz into a brothel, whorehouse, or general palace of ill-repute, waving his gun and strong arming the madam.

"Okay, pay up, toots!" (Perhaps he used stronger language, but I can't help but seeing the preceding scene as something from a James Cagney gangster epic from the thirties!)

"And what if I don't?" asked the square-jawed old whorehouse madam, her young stable of fresh fillies cowering behind the voluminous hems of her Victorian skirt.

The masked hoodlum snarled, "Why, then I'll take every last penny out of the pretty hides of your girlies here!"

And with that, he cracked the butt of the gun against the too-painted visage of a hovering whore, sending her sprawling to the dirty carpet in a bloody, weeping heap.

"All right! Enough!" yelled the madam, "I'll pay whatever you want! Just, *leave my girls alone, all right?*"

Of course, it was not long after that Gillis/Nelson or a confederate would return, promising protection against such strong arm tactics . . . at a price. It was in this way that Babyface first broke his way into the wonderful world of organized crime.

Nelson fell in love with a girl working the counter at Woolworth's, Helen Wawzynak, who was making a meager living selling hardware. Calling her his "Million Dollar Baby from the Five- and Ten-Cent Store," the relationship soon blossomed into a full-blown criminal romance, Wawzynak soon taking the roll of gangster's moll to heart. Nelson, for his part, was making a good living working for kingpin Al Capone, shaking down labor leaders and using familiar strong-arm tactics to consolidate Scarface's reign of terror.

(If a union leader was unceremoniously or accidentally dispatched by a beating turned too rough, well, it was all the same to Babyface, who took murder in its stride.)

Finally, even the cold-blooded killers of the Capone organization began to feel the utterly ruthless and insane Nelson was more of a liability than anything else, so they shit-canned him, causing him to return to his old job of demanding protection money from whorehouses and other "gentleman's clubs." It was 1928, the Depression was looming, and the rotting fruit of the American dream was overripe for the plucking by criminal hands.

Nelson participated in a jewelry heist (also reportedly a bank heist, but accounts conflict) that year. Perhaps he went in, with a mask over his face, a bandana, his six-shooter waved around casually as his bugging, burning eyes demanded "gimme da ice!" Maybe it was like this. Maybe life is like a Golden Age comic book or bad gangster movie from 1932.

Whatever the case, little Babyface went to the Big House. Here, his tempestuous, Napoleonesqe inner drive toward domination and destruction—his psychotic "short man's syndrome"—was buttressed by the abuse he suffered at the hands of fellow cons. Miracle the little bastard survived (for his victims, it might more properly be termed a *tragedy* that he managed to survive.)

His sentence had been one year to life—but Mr. Babyface didn't intend to stick around long enough to see if life behind bars would be his eventual, tragic fate. During a prison transfer, he escaped his guards, becoming a certified A-Number-One American Fugitive from justice. Mr. Gillis made tracks for far away (at least from Wheaton, Illinois) Reno, Nevada. From there, it was Sausalito. We might conjecture that his "Million Dollar Baby" followed him in close proximity.

It was in Sausalito that Babyface would meet John Paul Chase, his criminal counterpart. A somewhat chiseled, seedily handsome man (in the way such men of the 1930s projected a kind of off-brand matinee idol charm), the moustachioed Chase was a rum runner during the years of Prohibition. Recognizing in Babyface a tempestuous, ruthless, and seemingly fearless little bulldog, he took him on as a strong arm man to protect the liquor truck. And my, judging from the history of things, those ol' boys had a bloody good time.

For, in Minneapolis, t'was said a man was gunned down from a passing car, one with California plates. Chase later claimed Nelson killed another man in Reno (Johnny Cash fans will note this bears a striking similarity to a particular, popular song. We must assume Nelson did not do this, however, "just to watch him die.") a material witness in a mail fraud case. Whatever the case, it was chalked up as just one more bloody victory for Nelson.

Nelson had hit his first bank in Chicago as early as 1931. He had already been to boys' school for auto theft, among other things. He had whetted his appetite for blood. So, upon meeting Dillinger henchman Homer Van Meter, Nelson seemed to have blundered into a criminal match made in Heaven. Dillinger began to accompany Nelson and Van Meter to San Antonio on bank robbery expeditions. Chase, returning temporarily to California, left Nelson and wife to take a much-needed crime vacation at Little Bohemia campground in Wisconsin. Hence so transpired the very famous:

Raid on Little Bohemia

It was near Manitowish Waters, Wisconsin, off US Highway 51, when the FBI completely bungled the famous (or rather infamous) "Raid on Little Bohemia."

(This was on April 20. It has been noted that the April 20–April 30 "black corridor" sees the anniversary of many, many revolutionary and troubling events. Beginning with the "Shot Heard Round the World" in the American Revolution, this date sees the anniversary of such notable events as the first LSD trip [by a bicycling Dr. Hoffman], the birthdate of Adolph Hitler on April 20, 1891; the suicide of Adolph Hitler on April 30,1945, [incidentally, the ancient pagan holiday of *Walpurgisnacht*]; the birthdate of Vladimir Lenin on April 22, the birthday of Robert Oppenheimer, the "Father of the Atomic Bomb," on April 22, the famed Warsaw Ghetto Uprising on April 21st, the founding of the modern state of Israel on April 30, 1948, the founding of the Church of Satan on April 30, 1966 [it's founder Anton LaVey, was, incidentally, also born in April]; the Fall of Saigon during the Vietnam War; the OKC Bombing in 1994; the suicide of the Branch Davidian Cult at Waco in 1991; The Columbine High School Massacre in 1999; The LA Riots; The Virginia Tech College Massacre in 2005 . . . and, I'm certain this is not all. Also, May 1, the infamous "May Day", is an international holiday for Marxists and communists the world over. As I said, a troubling, revolutionary time of upheaval. Must be written in the stars. We also mention, in passing, that Lincoln was assassinated on April 15, 1865—but this is cheating the dates a little.)

The raid went down this way.

Dillinger and gang drove up to Little Bohemia, which was a motor lodging business founded by immigrant Mr. Wanatka. There drove a number of cars, and the assembled criminals including Dillinger, Van Meter, Pierpont, Billy Frechette, Nelson, his wife . . . pretty much the whole un-merry mess. They signed in under assumed names; what they told the proprietor as a cover for why their huge group was traveling together is anyone's guess. Outside, perhaps while Dillinger was signing the guest registers, the incessant barking of the guard dogs gave a sort of prescient warning of the melee that was to transpire.

Dillinger asked: "Can you put up ten guests?"

And Mr. Wantaka answered: "Sure enough. But, such a large company is a little unusual." Right away, the old man was a little suspicious.

"Johnny" smiled that weird, crooked little grin of his, trying to put the old man at ease. He said: "We're a church group."

(A little literary license can be forgiven.)

Behind the Little Bohemia campgrounds was a ravine bordering on Lake Eerie. Perfect escape route, it would seem.

It was a card game that first alerted Mr. Wanatka that his "guests" were, in point of fact, Babyface, Dillinger, and the whole motley crew. Mr. Wanatka was busy with a game of seven-card stud when he noticed Dillinger, who had won a sizable pot, was carrying a holstered sidearm. Johnny (who had thoughtfully taken to dying his hair red as a disguise) bent over to rake up his filthy lucre, thus exposing himself.

Mr. Wanatka, a hardworking immigrant, had married Mrs. Wanatka, who had once been a rum runner for her brother's illegal booze operation. He went into the back of the main lodge, got out a newspaper, nearly had a heart attack.

"I don't believe it! It's him! It's Dillinger . . ."

He put the paper down, his mind racing on what to do. Dillinger, Babyface, Van Meter . . . he (and everyone else in the United States at that point) knew these men to be cold-blooded killers. He knew, also, he couldn't risk a shoot-out in such close proximity to his family.

He went back out into the barroom, called Red in back.

He handed him the front page of the paper.

"You're John Dillinger," he said, point-blank. Johnnie good-naturedly smiled, knowing the jig was up.

"Sure. But, hey pops, were just here for a little rest and relaxation. We'll be gone shortly."

Mr. Wantaka, knowing he had little choice in the matter at this point, said, "Okay. I can't risk a shoot-out here. Every cop in the country is looking for you. All I own in the world, including my family, is right here. I won't say anything."

This was apparently good enough for Johnnie Dillinger, who made sure each member of the family was closely watched, all conversations conveniently monitored, nonetheless.

Mrs. Wanatka, after becoming informed of the situation, didn't like it one bit. What's more, she was convinced that the psychotic Babyface had been put on her trail as she took a trip to town. Which was indeed the case.

She managed to inform her sister. The two women conspired as to what to do.

The gang, spread between the main lodge at Little Bohemia, and the adjacent cottage, were becoming increasingly uneasy. Dillinger and Nelson tried to soften things up, be friendly; they played ball with Mr. Wanatka's little son, who complained that Nelson, the penultimate bully, threw the ball too hard, so that catching it hurt. Mr. Wanatka was becoming more and more unnerved.

His wife managed to contact her brother, slipping him a package of cigarettes with a note inside. He quickly went to the local FBI office, who just as quickly informed chief investigator and Dillinger nemesis Melvin Purvis.

This set the Illinois and Minnesota FBI offices in a frantic blaze, as they attempted to organize a raid on the roadside resort before Dillinger and company took it into their heads to blow. Purvis chartered a private plane; other agents, afraid to fly, went by car, etc., getting to their mustering point however they could. An emergency dispatch, a message sent on by Mrs. Wantaka to her brother, revealed that the agents had better act quick, as Dillinger was planning on becoming scarce earlier than expected.

"We'll be taking off this evening after dinner, Pops. So, you can relax now!" Dillinger said, trying to sound cheery; in reality, Johnnie was getting increasingly more nervous by the minute; "Pops" was having one of his famous "Dollar-a-Plate" dinner specials, and there were all kinds of people coming and going—"Too many people seeing us," Dillinger bemoaned. Nelson was probably still fuming at having been put in the adjacent cabin as opposed to getting the nicer lodgings in the main building ("We'll put him in the guest cabin!" the little outlaw had screeched.) but nonetheless decided it would probably be prudent to *amscray*. So be it, said Dillinger, they'd leave right after dinner at five.

Dinner was steak with garlic. (I wonder: do they mean "garlic bulbs"? Did they not have potatoes handy?)

Purvis and the massed G-Men commandeered a number of cars, one they rented outright from a man at the airport for a handful of dollars. Such were the methods of the Bureau in those bygone days.

One car broke down en route. Agents jumped out, got up on the running board of the accompanying car, and, in icy Wisconsin temperatures, in the middle of April, held on through the thick upward climb through the pine trees to Little Bohemia. It was altogether an ill-omened beginning to what would turn out to be a disastrous raid.

†

The man was slumped over the front seat of the car, bleeding profusely from his bullet wounds. The FBI agent who had opened fire on him came forward to examine the body.

To his horror, he discovered that the man was not one of the notorious gangsters they had come gunning for. Matter of fact, it was a local peon from the Federal Work Camp, another luckless Depression-Era laborer who had come aboard the New Deal, looking for employment. Instead, an idle night eating and drinking his paltry earnings away at the Little Bohemia had now cost him an early grave.

The errant agent, Carter Baum, swore later that he could never fire his gun again. Notwithstanding this promise, Purvis held his ground, certain that Nelson and Dillinger were inside the encampment. (They had likewise fired on a lesser gangster and his moll as they had driven up, but the duo managed to elude the law officers.)

All of the gunfire had alerted the wanted men hiding inside. A battle ensued, with men running to the back windows of the lodge, exchanging fire with agents. Unbeknownst to the agents, these men didn't hunker down when gunfire erupted back at them, but, in the confusion, managed to slip down on a huge outcropping of dirt and slide unnoticed into the woods, down the trails edging the lake. Babyface, predictably, after firing his salvos at the G-Men, went the wrong way, completely contravening the Dillinger Escape Plan, with him and his taking off crosswise through the dark and confusion of the woods while Dillinger and his cohorts drove the other route, finally ending up at the home of a terrified elderly couple.

"I wouldn't hurt a hair on your heads," Johnnie assured the square citizenry. And he kept his word. "We just need a place to repair for a little while."

Nelson, on the other hand, had *no* such compunctions about killing. As if to prove this, he drove directly to a home owned by a local police dispatcher. Outside, G-Men, led by the still-grieving Carter Baum, were sitting in a car, waiting for Nelson, or Dillinger, or somebody from this botched goddamned raid to surface. Nelson was trying to steal a car at the moment, and, obviously annoyed by the interruption, grabbed his subgun and strolled up to the tragically-fated law officers.

"I know you guys wear bullet proof vests!" he roared. "So, I'll give it to you high and low!"

He did.

†

Melvin Purvis and the entire United States law enforcement apparatus suffered a *massive* black eye due to the infamous botched raid at Little Bohemia. Dillinger and Babyface were now Public Enemies Numero Uno and Dos . . . Dillinger, after buying it at the Biograph Theater in Chicago (executed by Officer Martin Zarkovich while in the company of German—*ahem*—"procuress" Anna Sage, the infamous "Woman in Red"). One of Johnnie's distant descendants has told me they charged a penny a piece to view the body. I dunno, but that seems logical.

In a day before television and the Internet, seeing the body of an infamous gangster was a rare treat for a growing kid or his slack-jawed, drudge-like parentage (am I being harsh?). Vide the displays made of Bonnie and Clyde, Jesse James, and even the pickled noggin of Mexican bandito Joaquin Murieta, whose severed head was preserved in a bell jar and was an essential piece of the collection of an Old West afficiando for time out of mind. Johnnie assumed room temperature on July 22, 1934 (mystic significance, quite possibly, in the numbers 7-22. Seven is a no-brainer; 22 is simple 11 + 11 . . . and the eleven-eleven combination is considered significant by those who happen to glance at their digital clocks on the same exact readouts twice daily. Of course, there is more to it than that. Curiously, as I was writing this part of the chapter, I picked up a sheaf of papers my grandmother had left me before going into nursing care. One of them was a reproduction of the front page of the *Marion Chronicle Tribune*, announcing that JOHN DILLINGER IS SLAIN!)

By the time Babyface made his way out to Arizona in a stolen car, most of his criminal compadres had found out just what the Shadow meant when he laughed sardonically and announced that "Crime Does Not Pay!" Homer Von Meter was gunned down by vigilantes after breaking down in a blind alley. John Hamilton was dumped rather unceremoniously in an abandoned stone quarry after his corpse was bathed in carbolic acid, to try and foil investigators; he died a lingering, miserable death from an untreated bullet wound, BTW.

And the above listed were not the only gangsters to meet foul ends; *all* of them were being shit-canned by fate and their own stupidity, the "evil that men do" catching up with them. They became so many shocking morgue photographs, their final stab at eternal infamy lost on the immovable shocked mannequin visages displayed in gory relief for all and sundry (with a penny?) to come and gawk at for a few moments.

Nelson knew he was going to get it in the end. The only question was when. After hearing how Johnnie got *his*, he decided to move ever further west, to sunny Cali, to lay low and draw up plans.

He didn't lay long. The demon reared up in him, and the little bastard got edgy, antsy to get back in the game, though he knew, surely, it would be the death of him.

"I'm gonna hit a bank a *week* for a solid month, ya hear me?"

They heard. At this point, they were limited strictly to Mrs. Babyface Nelson and flunkie John Paul Chase; everyone else was dead or behind bars. Nelson and company came back to the Midwestern world of long, flat farm fields, rotting barns, pissant burgs a block long, and little small town banks, just ripe for the plucking.

And this is where the story ends, and simultaneously, crosses over into the legendary.

Nelson and companions were driving near Fox River Grove, Illinois, on November 27, 1934. It was Helen and Chase with him. Two G-men spotted them, identified Nelson, and gave chase. A wild gun battle ensued, with shots flying here, there, and yonder. Nelson braked near the town of Barrington, jumped from his car with Chase, and Helen went and hid in a nearby wooded area.

The agents, Hollis and Cowley, hid behind their car and exchanged fire with the two outlaws, Nelson returning fire with his Browning assault rifle. Chase was wounded and dove into a ditch.

Nelson was wounded. And wounded. And wounded. However, like a ski-mask wearing slasher out of some cheap horror flick, he absolutely *refused* to lay down and die. Perhaps he was a distant cousin to Rasputin.

He took a licking . . . well, you know the rest.

"With his eyes blazing and blood in his teeth, the maniacal, cold-blooded little man came forward across the hot stretch of Illinois highway, his gun blazing before him, blood dripping from numerous wounds all over his form. Sweat and blood and tears streamed in a squalid, repulsive mixture down his smooth, moon-like chins, as he gritted his teeth and croaked to himself, 'I'll take you all to Hell with me!'"

The above passage is a hypothetical, imaginary passage from a book I will never write fictionalizing the life of George Lester Babyface Gillis Nelson. Or maybe I am channeling some old, dead pulp fiction hack. No matter. Babyface finally collapsed.

His final photo, laid out on the morgue slab with a string of intestines hanging from his mutilated torso, is actually quite telling. Some would say Nelson was finally at peace, others that he looked as if he were suppressing a final laugh.

I have no opinion, either way.

CHAPTER 15

Mark of the Assassin

Charles Julius Guiteau

(Note: Since it is the first priority of the author to never be boring, I offer the first little vignette of this chapter to you in the hopes that it might drag from you, oh dour and lugubrious peruser of true crime literature, the ghost of an ironic smile. That it concerns itself, in its own way, with the subject of a presidential assassin is self-evident; whether or not it is in good taste or not should also be self-evident. I offer it here, simply because I *can*.)

†

The copious vomit drip, dripped down from the theater box. Behind him, John Wilkes Booth was still trying to pull the trigger on a brace of bananas some unthinking poltergeist had replaced his pistols with. Mary Todd bounded out of her chair, and, being exceedingly flatulent, broke explosive, ectoplasmic wind, as the people seated to the left and right of the Lincolns strained to hear the dialogue coming from the stage.

"Oh, I do wish that the president would halt that infernal racket, and Mrs. Lincoln, too. For, I have long waited to see Our American Cousin!" whispered the wife, but, loudly enough that Booth could hear them over the gagging, flatulating, and squish of his banana gun.

"Drat," cried the erstwhile assassin, and, flinging the overripe fruit aside, yelled "*Sic Semper Tyrannus*!" waving his fist in the air, and bounding from the theater box to the vomit-streaked stage.

Audience members, not alerted to the full tragedy that was occurring just above, exclaimed, "What did that poor man yell? Did anyone catch it?"

And one man said, "Sounded like 'Sick pimple moronis.' I suppose I could be mistaken, though."

And his wife said, "No, no, he quite clearly said 'Distemper tie shamus.' I heard it distinctly. Whatever *that* means!"

And one old codger, missing teeth and chewing a wad of tobacco exclaimed, "Ha! You're both wrong! What that varlit said was 'Enter sick into my anus.' Anus! Anus, I tells ya! That man said the word *anus* . . ."

And most thought the old codger was quite mad, after hearing this ejaculation.

Booth bounded to the stage. The legend, of course, being that he broke his ankle in the jump. However, as historians in the know know, this is patently *wrong*. He actually slipped in Lincoln's vomit, which was how he twisted the ankle, and why he limped away, into the night.

In another part of town Herold was leading another assassin, whose name the author has temporarily misplaced, to the home of Secretary of State Seward, who was healing up after trying to masticate a coconut whole. (Which, according to the infernal logic of politicians, made perfect sense, as the coconut, being a symbol of Caribbean living, was undoubtedly and indubitably there to be conquered by the noble Euro-American piesucker.)

He was laid in a contraption worthy of the Marquis De Sade, a nightmare of metal pins and leather straps, but he could manage to ask for "thinner," and "foffee," and, occasionally, a "Ffficar to moak!"

The men rode up to the door, Herold doing the bravest act he could muster at the time and disappearing without a trace into the night. The erstwhile assassin, Mr. Lewis Paine, rode up to the door, but was dismayed when the butler told him he couldn't take his beloved horse inside.

Mr. Paine quietly went up the stairs, encountering only Seward Junior as he went.

"May I help you, sir?" was the curt inquiry.

Mr. Paine decided that telling the son he was here to kill his father would be rather bad form, so instead he confessed, "Oh, I'm here selling magazine subscriptions. I need to see your dad. I heard he's an enthusiastic fly-fisherman."

The son frowned, grimaced, rolled his eyes, clucked his tongue, puffed out his cheeks, scratched his chin, walked about in a circle, (well, really, I think you get the point about his personal tics and idiosyncratic behaviors), and said, "No! No! No! I'll have you know that papa hasn't been fly fishing, skeet shooting, hot air ballooning, hang-gliding, or auto racing in, oh, a great many years!"

And Mr. Paine thought this peculiar. Scratching *his* chin, he said, as if in self-reflection, "Auto racing? Auto racing? What the hell does *that* mean? Outta my way, man!"

And, suddenly losing patience, he pushed past Seward Junior, bounded up the stairs, and went down to the end of the hall, where a young girl, presumably the daughter, was bent low, whispering into a keyhole.

"Papa, oh papa, what big teeth you have!"

And the muffled answer from within came: "Feebedde do fee you wiff, by dear!"

And then: "Papa, oh papa, what big eyes you have!"

And the reply: "Feebedda do daste you viff, by dear!"

And then: "Papa, oh papa, what big ears you have—"

Mr. Paine, wondering what sort of madhouse he had stumbled into, pushed the girl aside and said, "Girl! Stand aside! I am here to kill Secretary of State Seward and strike a blow for the late, great Confederate State! Hah! Yass 'um! Yass 'um! The South will rise again, missy! Now, just try and stop me!"

And, since she did nothing to try and stop him, he spat, cursed, and kicked the door open.

He was surprised when Seward himself came out, his head wrapped in bandages and pins and screws sticking out of his face.

"Gan I elp ooo?" he mumbled.

At this, Paine reached for his gun, and was surprised when he pulled out, instead, a large kielbasa.

He paused before commenting, "Some idgit has gone and replaced my sidearm with a sausage!" But, knowing he had to make the best of things, he took the sausage and began to furiously whip Secretary of State Seward around the head and shoulders, shouting, "En guarde! Take that, and that! And some of that! And some more of that!"

And Mr. Seward threw up his arms, and began to cry "Elp! Elp! Murfer! Murfer! Ohmycod, elp!" Before falling to the floor, not even mildly injured.

Mr. Paine beat a hasty retreat, thinking, "I'll hook up with John Wilkes Booth to make my escape. It's the safest bet."

As for Mr. Axerodt, who was to slay Vice President Johnson, he sort of hemmed and hawed, walked around town, looked at his watch, stopped for a bite, felt his bowels grow increasingly watery at the prospect of all the trouble he was going to get into for being a presidential assassin, and got a case of the dribbling runs quite unlike anything he had ever experienced before.

And, of course, when you need to find a public restroom, one hadn't even been invented yet.

"It all seemed like fun and games when we was planning it out, of course. I remember Mrs. Surrat poking her head into our secret meetings, saying things like, 'What are you boys doing in there? You boys aren't planning any bold historical or revolutionary acts, are you?'

"And I'd always pipe up and say, 'Well, we sure aren't planning on assassinating Abraham Lincoln, if that's what you mean!' But, of course, that's what we were doin'!"

And, because he realized he was merely talking to himself, he suddenly shut up.

"Well, you all can take all the glory for yourselves, see. And all the grief, too. Yeah, that means you Mr. Booth, Mr. Surrat, Mr. Paine, Mr. Herold! I'm out of here!"

And, still chattering to no one in particular but himself, he climbed up on his horse and, indeed, was out of there.

Of course, they were all captured and hung. Mrs. Surrat, too; and she was the nation's first female executed by federal authority. It was a historical footnote I'm very sure she would happily have done without being the subject of.

The resulting photo is intensely creepy, Mrs. Surrat being hung in her long black dress, with her legs tied together and a sack over her head. If we pull back from the scene of the conspirators getting ready to take a short dance at the end of a long rope, we might see a young man, this author, holding a copy of Bloodletters and Badmen, sitting on the porch of a friend's house. The house was on an old Indiana road in the country, and although it had all the most modern attributes and conveniences, was quite old; and supposedly haunted, to boot.

Across a gravel drive was an abandoned cemetery, with folks buried there from before the Civil War. But all of this was twenty years ago.

†

The preceding digression was my only *other* piece of writing on the subject of presidential assassins, a subject I intend not to revisit very often, if at all. The parody (my first) amused me so much, I used the excuse to publish it here.

The very *real* presidential assassin we are going to tell you about, Charles Julius Guiteau, was an itinerant lawyer and wild eccentric who made his living taking on lawsuits for feckless, indigent clients. The suits were frivolous and often thrown out—the clients rarely saw any remunerative compensation for their trouble. Guiteau argued monstrously and absurdly, haranguing the court in a paranoid manner about the Lord, and His will—and also, presumably, about his own pesky creditors and landladies seeking back rent.

Most settlements were appropriated by the erstwhile attorney. Next on his mad agenda, the deflowering of a sixteen-year-old waif (I am uncertain as to the man's age at this point, but am reasonably comfortable in assuming he was, at least, old enough to be this girl's father).

He impregnated the luckless lass, soon abandoning her on the mean streets of Washington, DC. The year, I might say, was 1880, and former President Lincoln had only been in his grave for sixteen years.

Mr. Guiteau, after having sloughed off his tragic child bride, became interested in the attentions of outright whores, and developed for himself the then-fatal disease syphilis, which slowly drove him mad (madder? More mad?).

It was then that, like other men before him (and after him; some of our contemporaries, if you take my meaning), decided that the world owed him . . . something for his genius. He decided that this something, for untold reasons, was an ambassadorship to Paris. He decided to run down to 1400 Pennsylvania Avenue to have a word with the president about this situation.

The president at the time was James A. Garfield. He was the twentieth president of the United States. The year was 1881.

†

It is perplexing to note that, even though Lincoln had been killed a scant *sixteen* years earlier by a crazed bad actor in a crazed bad drama (that has resulted in any number of crazed, bad reenactments for stage and screen, by low-rent thespians under the direction of mediocre directors and money-grubbing producers), there was *no* Secret Service protection in sight, and Mr. Guiteau was allowed to roam *freely* into the White House, where he demanded, and obtained, a meeting with Garfield.

It rankled bitterly with the little, shrill psychopath that Garfield had neglected to use *his*, yes *his* speech—even though the pamphlet he published from that speech had, quite obviously, swayed the voting public into electing Mr. Garfield in the first place. Mr. Garfield was nonplussed apparently, and sent Mr. Guiteau on his way.

In the echoing (one imagines) hallways of the august, ancient building, Mr. Guiteau then accosted (daily) Secretary of State Blaine, who, in exasperation, finally exploded on the little man, exclaiming, "Never speak to me of the Paris Embassy again!" (At least, something to that effect.)

Mr. Guiteau felt a deep and sincere hurt at this point; one that he felt could only be alleviated by buying a .44 cal pistol and blowing Mr. President Garfield into Kingdom Come.

Thus, obtained he the firearm and practiced with it thusly: He shot the shrubbery along the Potomac. Then, he began to shadow the President's tour itinerary. This was not hard, as the daily newspapers actually *printed the president's movements* for any and all to see. (Ah! Things were so much more simple and trusting in that carefree, bygone era, so long ago . . .)

†

"God Told Me to Kill!"

It was July 1, 1881. It was the Baltimore and Potomac train station, and Mr. Guiteau (who by his own admission, had kept up a vigil that included watching Garfield enter and leave the White House from a park bench, and even trailing him to church, where he had considered shooting him down as he worshipped—but didn't, because, "that dear soul" Mrs. Garfield was with him) waited for the president and Secretary of State Blaine to disembark from the train en route to Mr. Garfield's alma mater of Williams College. Mr. Guiteau stepped forward and secured for himself a place in history—or maybe a footnote, at the very least.

Mr. Garfield was hit in the back, succumbing to his wounds later. Mr. Blaine survived, and Mr. Guiteau was quickly wrestled off to a Washington, DC jail, a place he would initially describe, after a short tour, as being "a fine place, a fine jail." (He confessed in court he had visited to see "what his future home would be like.")

Mr. Guiteau became a nine-day wonder, was put on a kind of Barnumesque display as he paraded, proud and arrogant, around the prison exercise yard. Jeering crowds came to see the killer, to goggle at a man so undeniably insane, yet so monstrously bold, as to shoot down the *president of the yoo ess eh . . .*

Like every psychopathic narcissist before or since, Mr. Guiteau seemed to truly love the attention.

His ten-week trial was, predictably, a circus.

Utilizing the theatrical methods that would be employed later by infamous cons such as Charles Manson, Guiteau frolicked like a madman in front of judge and jury. Calling them all stupid bastards, invoking the power and presence of "The Lord," and generally behaving as erratically and bizarrely as possible to the assembled witnesses. (At one point, he enjoined that they were "witless bastards," complete morons, and further confessed that it was his holy mission to kill President Garfield. Holy mission or not, fate or no, the jury was having none of it.)

His patina of insanity fell, legally speaking, on deaf ears and blind eyes: He was duly sentenced to hang. His final words included a laughable poem, giving a clue as to the divorced sense of reality he possessed. According to Jay Robert Nash, it included the line: "Halleluia, I am going to the Lordy."

CHAPTER 16

The Kingpin's Kingpin

The World of Capone

The following is an apocryphal story of Al Capone. It was featured in the book The 48 Laws of Power by Robert Greene, a book I admire *very* much. I can set the scene:

Count Victor Lustig got off the train, made his way carefully to the headquarters of a man that was, perhaps, the most respected and feared man in Chicago. He didn't have an appointment; he was taking a chance he would be let in to see the "Boss," a.k.a. Alphonse Capone.

He made his way past the glowering guards, men whom he knew, full-well, were capable of killing him. Inside, he waited for the Boss to see him, his cool, stony composure belying a man who made his living conning others. He had been in tough spots and dangerous jams before, and he had learned to "play it cool," always.

When confronted with the glowering Capone, Lustig confidently strode to his desk, and, with hat in hand, addressed the Boss thusly: "Mr. Capone, I've come to make you an offer you can't refuse. I am privy to some information . . ."

And so began the flinty "Count," a man with no more right to a noble title than Ronald McDonald. Capone sat back in his chair, a cold, inscrutable (and also terrifying) look playing across his famous scarred features. In short, the phoney-baloney Count offered him a sweetheart deal: If the Boss trusted him with ten grand of his own money, Lusting promised to *double* it . . . within six months.

"I promise you, Mr. Capone. It's a sure thing. You can't lose money on this, no way!"

Lustig, the very picture of poise and confidence, assured Scarface that he, indeed, was on the up and up. Capone, who figured he knew a con artist when he saw one, agreed anyway, peeling off the requisite capital and handing it over to Lustig. Capone probably figured that, if the man was simply a very bold or very stupid grifter, he would have fun cutting him into itty-bitty pieces when he came back empty-handed. Of course, if he decided to skip, well . . .

Capone knew he was taking a big chance. But, he grinned, perhaps enjoying the prospect of being conned a little. He handed Lustig over the ten G's, and the erstwhile Count, bowing, and doffing his hat, left amicably, elated that the notorious crime boss should have deigned to trust him.

The Count *also* realized he was taking a risk. Perhaps a fatal one. At any rate, he did *nothing* with the money, except rent a safety deposit box. Therein he placed the ten thousand and left town.

Six months later, he returned to Chicago, removed the money from the box, and returned to Scarface's headquarters. Escorted in to see Da Boss, Count Victor Lustig bowed deeply, took off his hat, placed it over his heart, and slowly began, "I–I regret to inform you that the plan . . . failed. I failed. I wasn't able to double your money."

Capone, who we might imagine was sitting behind his desk chewing a fat cigar when he heard the news, took the burning stogie out of his mouth, put it in the ashtray, growled, and, trying to determine how many pieces he would saw this charlatan into, began to speak.

Before the kingpin could utter a word, however, the Count opened his valise, and said, "I'm returning your money. Here it is, to the penny." He removed the ten thousand, put it on the desk.

Capone looked at Lustig, and then at the money. Suddenly, the old monster stood up, threw his hands into the air, and exclaimed, "By God, you're honest!"

Then he said: "You know, I know you're a con man. I knew it the moment you walked in here. I expected to get ripped off. But this? To get my money back?"

And with that, Scarface peeled off five grand and handed it to Lustig, saying, "Here. If you're on the spot, here's five bills to help you along."

The "Count" doffed his hat, thanked Capone for his munificent generosity, and walked out, $5,000 richer. He never intended, of course, to try and double Capone's money; the lesson from Robert Greene's book is that, occasionally, when you show honesty to a man who expects you to be a crook, he is so surprised he rewards you for your efforts, and you actually soften him for your "mark." Or, something like that.

†

Don't let the preceding narrative fool you into thinking Scarface ever exhibited anything less than the wiles of a curling python. One act of redemptive kindness doth not a saint make. A completely different Scarface emerges in a notable incident that happened at a place called the Hawthrone Ballroom. This incident was dramatized in the largely forgotten Kevin Costner vehicle from the eighties, the Scorcese-directed remake of the Untouchables, which also starred Sean Connery and Robert De Niro as Capone.

Capone invited his best henchmen to a fabulous dinner, linguini smothered in oily clam sauce, and red wine. The color of the wine was fitting.

The three unsuspecting guests of honor (unsuspecting in that, reputedly, the night would *not* turn out to be a celebration for them) sucked the delicious food down their windpipes, not realizing that these would be the last bites of food they would ever take while upon this earth, and Scarface, "Da Boss," strutted around the room, his tone becoming oddly more surly and more aggressive as he spoke.

"I owe these guys everything, lemme tell ya!" he said, but he didn't sound very sincere. "I tell you, with guys like these working for me, you know what I could get? Huh?"

He slapped some backs. We can visualize fat gangsters looking around rather nervously, pasta hanging halfway out of their mouths.

"Why, I'll tell you what I could get! *A bullet in the back of the head, that's what I could get.*"

And Scarface produced his trusty baseball bat. He lurked messeurs Scalise, Anselmi, and Giunta, striking first one, then the other, with homicidal blows, leaving their bleeding bodies to fall across the table. Which, of course, must have ruined the dinner for anyone else present.

The windows of the Hawthorne, of course, had been draped; all the better to keep the prying eyes of the law from peering in on the real life, honest-to-goodness, *not* from a James Cagney picture, MOB.

(I can be forgiven my literary license in regards to supplying the dialogue for the redoubtable Scarface, Kingpin of Prohibition-era crime. There *may* have been an enterprising, budding historian there taking a verbatim transcript, but I tend to doubt it.)

That incident happened in Cicero, Illinois, in 1929, only *seven* months after the infamous St. Valentine's Day Massacre, in which the three men Capone had just killed (they apparently made no move to defend their own lives; they knew, finally, it was hopeless) had committed the ultimate act for "Da Boss."

"You rats were gonna get me killed, huh? You were plotting against me?"

Capone's eyes were bulging; he was sweating profusely, as little fat men are wont to do when overtaxed by physical exertion. It was not, though, that Big Al was a weakling or wimp; not at all (as clearly attested to by the triple murders he had just committed). In fact, he had grown up, fist to jowl, since the moment of his unfortunate birth in 1899.

"Get them out of here!" Capone threw down his baseball bat, his imperial scepter as it were, a "hammer of the gods," or, in this case, "god," singular.

The year 1899. Alphonse Capone was born in Brooklyn to poor immigrant parents, in the hellish Williamsburg area, and quickly learned the basic, animalistic lessons of life that would carry him through until his death. He would alter nothing.

He became a member of the notorious "Five Points" gang, a one-man terror force enforcing the gang's will, muscling union leaders who refused to kick back some funds for the gang. He was really, really good at this.

Also, like Babyface Nelson, he could muscle the madams of various whorehouses. Money and dames and fast, violent adventure. Meting out the punishment, instead of taking it, as he had done since his birth. It was a heady, intoxicating mixture of violence and power.

But the "dago punk" (as his detractors called him) was still small time. He wanted more.

His compadres at this point included men like bosses Johnny Torrio and Joe Colisimo. Colisimo ran a network of whorehouses Capone was taxed to protect; perhaps act as a glorified bouncer. Colisimo liked the whoring business; he wasn't keen, though, on getting into bootlegging (after Prohibition came in); he didn't "understand" it (according to Jay Robert Nash) and, quite frankly, found it too dangerous.

Somehow this didn't sit well with Johnny Torrio and Lieutenant Capone; this mook was standing in the way of expansion, of progress—of "business."

"Joe, it's just business!" Torrio had tried to explain to the unyielding underworlder. Colisimo wouldn't budge on bootlegging; he had to be "rubbed out" of the equation.

"Them Wop Beerboys Fold Up Like Newspapers After One Chop!"

The above was among the declamations offered by one "Ragtime" Joe Howard, an old-fashioned gangster who neither carried a gun, nor thought he needed one. He would live (and die) to regret his lack of foresight.

Capone had no problem with killing. "Ragtime" Joe Howard had roughed up a Colisimo accountant for no good reason. Capone, hearing of this, decided it was not mete and good that such an affront should be allowed to go unpunished. It was just not good business.

Capone strutted into the speakeasy. Ragtime Joe, suddenly feeling a little watery in the guts, stuck out his hand, big as a dinner plate, and said "Hiya Al!" (curious for a man known to hate those of Italian descent, noting they "could be kicked around," pretty much at will).

Scarface was having none of it. He pulled his gun, emptied six shells point-blank into Ragtime's head, and calmly walked out. The three people at the bar, when questioned about the killing later, developed a funny blindness; they became unable to identify Al Capone as the killer of Ragtime Joe. Imagine that.

(People tasked with testifying against Mafioso are often shuttled into the modern "Witness Protection Program," which, of course, didn't exist in that bygone era.)

†

Al Capone died an inauspicious death.

Physically a "wreck," he has released after serving eight years of an eleven-year sentence at "The Rock," Alcatraz, the infamous prison said to be the home of many lost, wayward, suffering souls by legendary psychics, sleuths, ghost busters, and other such seekers after fame, fortune, and exploitative recognition. He was there while Robert Stroud, the "Birdman" was there, isolated from the outside world by waters said to be shark-infested. In truth, they just told the cons that to keep 'em guessing.

The Big Man, the "Dago Punk" that had proved himself to be a kingpin of crime, was now not so big. On Alcatraz, he was positively puny, sputtering around, paresis gripping a steadily-deteriorating brain. They say he put his pants on backwards sometimes.

All of this was due to Big Al forgetting to pay federal income tax . . . for a decade. What was he going to do? Credit his fifty-million-dollar fortune as the direct result of being in the "used furniture" business? (Note: Used furniture was one of Big Al's early fronts. His enemy, later victim, Irish Mobster Dion O'Bannion, likewise pretended to run a flower shop.)

Eliot Ness and his much-lauded "Untouchables" had moved Heaven and Earth (and furthermore seen the earth shoveled over a few of their enemies and compatriots), but, finally, it was the IRS that sent Al the Butcher to the Rock. Public outcry against the affable, if somewhat comically crude, cherubic gangland leader had reached a fever pitch, what with the nasty business on St. Valentine's Day, 1929.

"It Was Cops What Done It!"

Reportedly, these were the words, affixed above, uttered by a dying member of the Irish mob loyal to "Bugs" Moran, who laid low when he saw uniformed officers enter the garage at 2122 North Clark, on Chicago's Northside. Inside, seven men were there—the Dusenberg Brothers, Frank and Peter, who were both enforcers for Bugs Moran; Albert Kechelleck (alias "James Clark") second-in-command; Adam Heyer, a bookeeper; Dr. Rheinhardt Schwimmer, an optometrist who left the legit world because of an affinity for betting on horses; John May, a mechanic; and Albert Wienshenck, who managed phoney-baloney dry cleaning businesses for Moran, and who looked so much like Da Boss that it is believed he prompted the slaughter starting before Bugs even entered the building—out of mistaken identity, you understand.

The resultant carnage was sickening, devastating; maybe the surviving pictures don't do it justice. Thus quoth The Shadow: "Crime does *not* pay!"

The men were ordered up against the wall. Then, men, some dressed as cops, some wearing coats and hats, nice long trench coats—old-time gangsters from central casting—opened a volley of merciless fire, unceremoniously dispatching their hoodlum colleagues in an orgy of bloodletting that would go down in criminal history. Then they beat it—*amscrayed.*

The crook noses had been in the garage that day to drive a truck to Detroit—after stolen Canadian hooch. Witnesses saw a tell-tale black Sedan pull up to the building, describing two men dressed as regular cops—both carrying shotguns—and two other men dressed in their best gangster duds. All entered in back.

The weapon of choice for the slaughter were twin Thompson sub-machine guns. The blood-spattered bricks, incidentally, were said for years after (the garage was demolished in 1967) to be the result of bad fortune for whoever bought them to recycle. Urban legend, one supposes.

All in all, it was a coup for Scarface, who was now the undisputed potentate of the Chicago crime machine.

†

Perhaps we should touch on this a little.

There was a time in this country (presumably elsewhere, too) when various aspects of life—dating and relationships, marriage, business, politics, lunch counters, and even drinking fountains—were sharply divided along racial and ethnic lines. As puzzling as this is to us today, back in the early twentieth century, it was so . . . make of that whatever thou wilt.

(Of course, some would maintain that, even today, it is *still* mostly a game based on ethnicity and race—we just are no longer honest or open about it. I'm not giving an opinion on this.)

The world of organized crime was, likewise, heavily divided by intra-ethnic loyalties—as it were, the Italians, exemplified by the Brooklyn emigre Capone and his lieutenant, Torrio, controlled the Southside of Chicago. Meanwhile, a regular mook named Dion O'Bannion, who was of Irish ancestry, controlled, with such psychotic hair-trigger musclemen as William "Klondike" O'Donnell and his brothers, the Northside. East and West was up for grabs with various groups jockeying for position to get a "piece of da action."

A war of words had commenced between the two surly gangsters, Capone and O'Bannion. Capone considered O'Bannion soft in the head because he wouldn't run whores or open cat houses. "What, the guy has a problem with whores? What kind of a man doesn't like whores? It's business! BUSINESS!"

For his part, O'Bannion, who objected to whores, chiefly, through dint of his stern Catholic upbringing, thought of Capone as an "atheistical spaghetti-bender"; which, on the whole, doesn't sound very flattering.

(It should be noted that, likewise, Scarface referred to O'Bannion privately as "that phony, church-going turkeyneck!" Rubber and glue, I guess . . .)

Of course, a 1924 organized crime summit, attended by all interested parties, had carved up the territories satisfactorily for all sides. Hence, there was a sort of uneasy "peace" for awhile. But, there is no honor among thieves, and so the smouldering tensions between the two ethnic factions of Chicago's gangland life were always simmering below the surface, waiting to explode in a bloody nightmare of terror.

Colisimo had certainly found out how passionate Scarface could be on the subject of "hooers . . ."

Carrie Nation and her Bible, and her Women's Christian Temperance Union, had marched Prohibition, via a wave of exultant moralism, into public policy, forcing thirsty men to take their last drink on midnight, January 15, 1920, and enabling money-hungry mobsters to step in and fill the void left by Prohibition on the nation's beer-besotted soul.

It was the Jazz Age, the Flapper Age; the Charleston shaked and shimmied, movies were still silent, Gloria Swanson and Joan Crawford were competing over who had the hottest commodities on the silver screen. The Kennedys ran rum, Capone handled cheap Chicago brew, bathtub gin drove men blind and mad. God was in *his* heaven, amen.

The "Micks" controlled the North Side, the "Wops" the South. A veritable Murderer's Row of cold-blooded hitmen enforced the demarcation lines, maintaining ethnic parity for a short while. Alas, such uneasy alliances are bound to be violated eventually, by one side or another.

Capone, known for his violent temper (he once pistol-whipped a man after nearly ploughing into his vehicle, an accident that would have been Scarface's drunken fault) and Torrio had "300 gunsels" at their beck and call, ready to battle at the drop of a Homburg.

To keep it short and sweet, Capone's mob was dealing the death blow, here and there, sending men like the O'Donnell brothers to an early grave. Big Jim Colisimo had already been rubbed out by Scarface himself, shot to death in the lobby of one of his favorite eateries. Scarface and Johnny T cried like a couple of finnochios when the cops dragged them in for questioning—"Oh, Big Jim! Who in the hell would want to kill Big Jim, I ask you? Such a sweet, sweet man!" That sort of thing.

At any rate, they must have bought off the cops, because neither of them were ever prosecuted for that particular atrocity. It would not be long after that Johnny T himself would "get it"—but not fatally.

While standing in a phone booth, some men drove up. They were brandishing rifles. *Rat-a-tat-tat!* went the Browning (maybe Thompson) submachine guns, blowing the glass out of the phone booth and seriously injuring Capone's lieutenant. Johnny T got the message. *Amscray.*

He left Chi-Town for good, leaving "da business" to "Da Boss." Da Boss was now undisputed master of his little, sordid, blood-soaked, but undeniably profitable domain.

Capone eighty-sixed most of the O'Donnell clan, of the rival ethnically-Irish mob. Taking over their territory, he quickly also moved to install whorehouses in territory belonging to Irish mob rival Dion O'Bannion.

"Turkeyneck" O'Bannion, the "phony holy roller," didn't see this in a very favorable light; thus, he instigated a simmering, brutal war that left his rivals as well-dressed cadavers. Turkeyneck was an unhappy man at this point.

Pontificating to his underlings while filling claypots of geraniums full of rich, black Illinois dirt, he said, "It was all that dago punk! Those killings weren't on Torrio's orders! That dirty, atheistic dago! Did you see Jerry O'Connor's face at that funeral! Half of it blown off . . ."

Present were a few O'Bannion underlings, the most important of whom was the redoubtable (and undeniably psychotic) "Little" Hymie Weiss. Remember that name.

O'Bannion said, to a presumable Capone lieutenant/spy: "You can tell Capone that if he ever tries anything like that with us, I'm going to get him if I have to kill everyone in front of him to do it!" He furthermore added that the "greaseball" killed "like a beast in the jungle." Maybe he spit on the floor in disgust afterward, too. But, alas, we don't know.

What we do know is that, according to underlings, Capone was unnerved by O'Bannion's threat. O'Bannion was not like the O'Donnells, cheap hoodlum killers. He was a powerful, class act, with politicians and policemen on the take, the center of a powerful criminal enterprise with a lot of clout.

In the eternal struggle for power, control, and greater and greater pieces of the gangland pie, Scarface was at a momentary loss. What to do? What to do?

†

O'Bannion had devised a plan to get those "spaghetti-benders" even before Torrio checked out of the scene. He called up "Johnny Papa," told him he was selling off his Siebens brewery, and oh, would he happen to be interested?

For 500 G's, Johnny Torrio was interested. He paid cash. Five days later, the joint was raided by crooked cops on the O'Bannion payroll. It was the first salvo in an escalating, comically violent power struggle, and it was enough to send Scarface over the edge.

To add insult to injury, "Deanie" O'Bannion had been raiding Genna beer trucks—"To hell with those Sicilians!" he'd said, when an underling waxed philosophic that such an untoward move might, conceivably widen the already widening gulf between ethnic organized crime factions.

This was the straw that broke Capone's wildly insecure and paranoid ego. To rob them was one thing, but this was blood and honor they were talkin' now. O'Bannion, as far as Capone was concerned, was a *dead man.*

†

To that end, November 8, 1924, three dapper killers, Albert Anselmi, Jon Scalise, and transplanted Gotham gangster Frankie Yale, walked casually into the O'Bannion flower shop front, where the old man was busily trimming chrysanthemums.

"Hiya boys! You here for Frankie Merlo's wreath?" said the strangely unsuspecting gangland leader.

Fortuitously, the leader of the Unione Sicilian had just passed on, and every gunsel in a twenty-mile radius was busily sending flowers and condolences. Thus, the old man, who always carried not one, not two, but *three* guns concealed on him at all times, thought nothing of three crook noses sauntering in at one time.

These men were not there to collect a funeral wreath for Frankie Merlo. In a few moments, the man who formerly sold daises would be forever pushing them upward.

Yale took the old man's hand. The other two mooks came up beside O'Bannion, firing rapidly. The old man hit the floor of the shop, spilling flowers and blood everywhere. Yale bent over him, firing more rounds. Just to make sure.

Then the three dapper destroyers walked out, just as they had come in. Casually. No rush.

†

Hymie Weiss, whose devotion to O'Bannion was near-fanatical, vowed to see Capone, Torrio, and everyone else involved in his faction of the syndicate—"Dead! Dead! Dead!"

To *that* end, he settled sights on Torrio, first.

"Bullet's . . .tipped with garlic!" This quote came from Torrio. Hymie Weiss, a one-man vengeance machine that had sworn to take down the Capone mob in retaliation for the assassination of Dion O'Bannion, called up Scarface one happy, sunny day, and demanded he hand over Messeurs Anselmi, Scalise, and Yale. Capone bluntly told Weiss where he could go and what he could do there, adding, "I wouldn't do that to a yellow dog!" Meaning, he wasn't going to turn over his assassins.

Johnny Papa Torrio was leaning into the front window of his car one night, speaking with his wife, when she suddenly piped up about a car full of gunsels that pulled up besides them. "Rifles!" she peeped.

Before Johnny Papa could respond, the bullets started flying. Hit once, hit twice, Johnny Papa went down, bleeding badly. By the time the ambulance got there, he was barely conscious, but *still alive*. He croaked to the ambulance attendant, "Bullets . . . tipped with garlic!" And then he passed out.

But he lived.

But he decided to make tracks for Italy.

He and the wife were going on permanent vacation. Hymie Weiss, he figured, wouldn't follow him all the way across the Atlantic Ocean.

Be that as it may, Weiss wasn't done yet.

†

Capone's citadel in Cicero, the Hawthorne Hotel, seemed to be the perfect place for him to unwind, relax, and occasionally mete out murderous justice at the end of a Louisville Slugger. He and lieutenant Frankie Rio were eating in the restaurant one fine day (September 20, 1926) when all of a sudden, hearing a commotion down the street, Capone jumped up, yelling "Typewriters!"

Then both dove under the table (presumably everyone else in the place did, too). Rio told Da Boss, "Don't fall for it! This is just the bait to get you outside, so they can get a clear shot at you!"

He was right. Amazingly, in a scene that no Hollywood scriptwriter would dare dream up, the undeniably unhinged and murderously vengeful Hymie Weiss came riding into the Chicago suburb with *eight* cars of men, and all guns blazing. One almost imagines him standing on the hood, surfing in on an old-fashioned auto like some sort of felonious William Wallace, leading his troops into battle.

Rat-tat-tat-tat-tat!

Amazingly, miraculously, *no one was killed that day.* After the gunsels had ridden off into the sunset, a shell-shocked Scarface wandered through the bullet-riddled remains of his hotel; every window in the place had been blown out.

Suddenly, the Kingpin exploded in a towering rage. "They're dead, do ya hear me! All of 'em! Dead! Dead! *Dead*!" One imagines him swinging his arms comically, his chins quivering in spasmodic anger. Such was the road to the St. Valentine's Day Massacre, paved with spent shell cartridges. (My, how them twenties roared!)

†

Not a few days ago, I saw an article about Capone on the Internet. It was pretty basic, actually, hardly an article— just a shot of one of his prison cells, the pen he was incarcerated in right before being sent up to The Rock (Alcatraz).

It was pretty naff. Oh, the cell itself looked like a cave; maybe the walls were less cave-like all those decades ago, I don't know. But he had what looked like a Victrola, a rollaway desk, a comfortable bed, plush chairs . . . gangster furnishings, all crammed into a tiny, ugly, dank, and distressing prison cell. He used his influence. Even behind bars, he was still "Scarface."

More instructive is the old, forgotten gangster movie I remember seeing as a kid. In it, an old Sicilian godfather is sitting by a pool, looking like a rumpled mess. Two of his underlings are standing talking, saying, "It sure is a shame what has happened to Da Boss, huh?" I can't quote it exactly, of course, but you get the drift.

The man sitting by the pool let out a steady stream of bizarre, incoherent gibberish. Obviously a mental case. Granpa turned to me, said, "I think that's supposed to be Al Capone."

Released from prison after eleven years, Capone died of syphilis in 1947, a powerless shadow of his former self. He was *forty-eight*. Crime does not pay.

During his life, it is estimated he ordered the assassination of 500 men, with up to 1,000 being killed as a result of his Prohibition-era struggle for criminal dominance.

There is no word indicating if he put his pants on right-side-out the day he died.

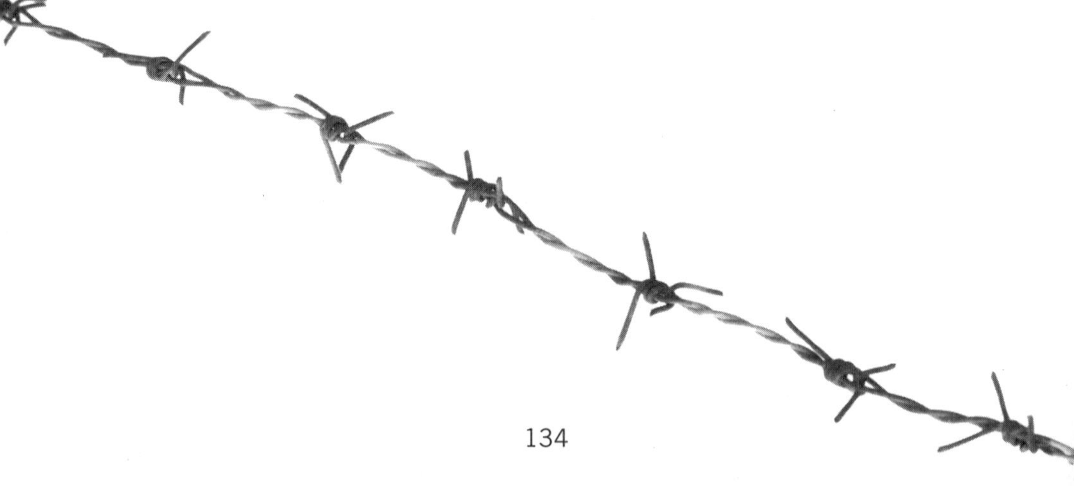

CHAPTER 17

The Nebraska Fiend

Stephen D. Richards

(Note: I was originally under the impression that the story of killer Stephen D. Richards was a contemporary, or at least, somewhat modern case. However, I was in no way disappointed by the fact that it actually took place in 1878. It is still a rather riveting account.)

If old-timey serial slayer Stephen D. Richards was calloused to the plight of human kind; if, in fact, he learned, as is later believed, to even take pleasure in inflicting suffering and pain upon his fellow man (and woman), then he probably received the lions' share of his education in cruelty, sadism, and callous indifference while fulfilling his obligation as undertaker in a brutal Victorian mental asylum.

An insane asylum, at that period in history, was a stark, hellish enough place without having to deal with the flow of dead bodies that, inevitably, were cast out from such a macabre institution. We imagine that all of the bodies were buried in unmarked graves; mayhaps, a lucky anthropologist may, some sunny day, dig up those moldering bones. About his stint as undertaker at the madhouse, Mr. Richards later had this to say:

> That took away to some extent my feeling and sympathy for mankind. I could stand by a man and see him die with no more feeling than I would have for a hog. When I left there . . . I didn't care for anything and had no respect for human nature.

Indeed, we can picture filthy, gape-mouthed patients marinating in stews of their own urine and feces, sleeping on lice-infested mattresses, strapped to beds or gurneys, locked in "Judas Cradles" (boxes with bars and lids that closed on top), and generally being abused to the point where, as opposed to the living hell on Earth in which they were condemned to reside, death probably seemed like a welcome respite. Into this world, psychopath Richards went, dipping his hand arms deep in the filth of dead lunatics, generally learning to be one callous sonofabitch.

But maybe we are getting ahead of ourselves.

An Omaha rag claimed a birthdate for him of 1836. He himself said he grew up during the Civil War. The dates would be all wrong. Born in Ohio, sometime in March, he traveled through various states with Ma and Pa, finally settling, as a man, on Nebraska. It was here (or so the confused, incomplete history of Mr. Richards would attest) that Stephen D. Richards decided to plant roots.

Bloody roots.

†

He seems to have had a strong desire to inflict punishment on mankind. His first murder was of a traveling companion, a man with whom he had pitched a camp.

The man said, "Don't ever say that again! It's a good thing you don't mean everything you say!" (At least, I take it that it was something to that effect. Maybe Richards had said something about his mother, sister, or lover; maybe Richards had intimated that his mother might likewise be his sister *and* his lover—an altogether more insulting suggestion. Whatever the case, Richards was having none of it.)

Mr. Richards replied, "Oh, but I *do* mean it! I mean it! I mean it very, very much!"

Whatever the hell it was Richards had said and meant, it caused quite a stir in the evening. According to his confession later, the irate companion went for his weapon (gun? knife?), but Richards was too quick, too snake-like for him. He blasted the man clean away with his own gun, a .33 and then beat a hasty retreat from Iowa. Or Nebraska (accounts vary). The year might have been 1878; the murdered man (whose name Richards could not recount) might have been twenty years old.

In 1878, having come to Kearney, Nebraska, via his constant wanderings, Richards was jailed on a minor offense. Therein, a man named Harelson and an accomplice (credited in accounts as either Underwood or Nixon!) managed an escape from jail with his help.

Mrs. Harelson (reportedly also incarcerated for a short period) was inestimably thankful to Richards, and, well, *ahem* . . . invited him to come visit her and her small brood anytime he might like to. (One can read between the lines here, the author supposes.)

Mr. Harelson, by the way, was in Texas, hunkered down against the authorities, who were looking for him long and hard.

Speaking of "long and hard . . ."

Mrs. Harelson, like some saloon floozy in an old Western picture, might have raised the hem of her skirt, revealing black fishnet stockings and a garter. Or she might have been decidedly more circumspect; either way, we feel Richards must have got the point. Perhaps he cocked a stupid, pathetic, toothless grin, scratched his stubbly face, and then took off his hat, and, holding it in both hands, pledged his undying fealty to La Harelson. There is no record of him doing this, but, just as assuredly, there is testimony to the fact that he began visiting the putative grass widow frequently.

Then, surveying her homestead with a true eye as to the value and comfort of such a place, he began to prevail upon her to sell him the property. Which, unbelievably (or perhaps, believably; maybe the woman was frightened of Richards, eager to join her husband, or maybe his sociopathic wiles simply got the better of her. Who can say?) she agreed to do.

It was on November 8th or 9th that he decided to murder the entire family with a hatchet. This consisted of Mrs. Harelson, her two daughters, and an infant. The infant he was later accused of smashing against a wall—bringing to mind Sawney Beane, Micahjah and Wiley Harpe, and Albert Fish's personal obsession with the Biblical verse: "Blessed is he who smashes his infant's head against a rock." (Psalm 137: 9) Whatever *that* is supposed to mean.

Disposing of the bodies (burying them on the property), he took a short leave to try and pawn off some of his victims' valuables before coming back, paying off any outstanding debts Mrs. Harelson possessed, and moving comfortably into his new digs. He rebuffed what niggling questions curious neighbors had by telling them that Mrs. Harelson and her uncommon (for the time) single-parent home had "gone west." Sure.

And maybe he would have continued this way for a long time, if it hadn't been for the pesky interference of a certain blonde bohunk named Anderson.

†

We might imagine a Nebraska Swede out of an old novel. Or, perhaps one could see him as a hulking brute straight from Erich Von Stroheim's 1924 silent epic Greed (based on the so-happy classic of American Naturalism McTeague, penned by Frank Norris in 1899), the huge, curly-haired dentist cum murderer portrayed by actor Gibson Gowland. In that film, McTeague bites the fingers of his neurotic, abused wife Trina (played with mystic exquisiteness by the incomparable Zasu Pitts), causing them to be amputated. Then, later, he murders her.

But, in the case of the blonde Swede Anderson (assuming he was blonde for no other reason than it suits our imagination) *he* was the one destined to be murdered.

He became quite chummy with his new neighbor.

His new neighbor returned in kind. He offered him a plate of food one fine day.

"Mmm, corn, potaters, hamhocks, lima beans . . . boy, you sure know how to treat a fellow, Stephen!"

"Aye! I hope you enjoy. Every. Single. Bite."

Mr. Anderson did indeed. But, funnily enough, later he started not feeling so good.

He scratched his head. He ran to the outhouse. He crawled into his bunk, moaning and groaning. He became very, very ill. He lingered on the edge for a short time (foreshadowing of what was to come).

"Sumbitch has poisoned me. That's all there is to it. He's still steamed over that argument we had about boundary rights. And he meant to do me in over it!"

Mr. Anderson recuperated slowly. Maybe he took some sort of tonic, maybe swallowed Castor Oil or syrup of ipecac to induce vomiting. Most likely, like the tough-as-nails folks of his own era, his body simply refused to give into the poisoned provender. Alas, it would fall to his wagging tongue, and the naked physical brawn of Richards, to accomplish what the homicidal repast had not: namely, the death of Mr. Anderson.

†

"Stephen, I know we've been friends for a long time . . ." began Anderson, eyeing the larger man warily.

Stephens replied, "Not really. Not so long."

Anderson seemed not to notice the implied sarcasm, but continued, "But, sometimes, things happen that a man just has to confront. This is one of those times. Now, I know'd you done put somethin' in my vittles t'other day, them that you served me. And I promise you, my friend, I'll go to the sheriff and tell him all that has occurred and what you did. Unless, of course, you can see fit to make up for your wrongdoing."

Stephens laughed, spat, said, "Anderson, you've gone clean out of your mind! What you got was a bellyfull of beans and a bellyache to go along with it. No surprise, you lily-livered, yellow-dog cur! But, tell me: Just what did you have in mind to buy with your silence? You want my fields, my land? Well, that's just not going to pass muster, I'm afraid."

Stephens slowly picked up a club. He brought it around from behind his back, slowly, circling his victim in a sort of casual, predatory manner. Anderson was so stunned by the sudden change in Stephens' disposition that the one thing that could have saved him, turning and running, was *not* something he chose to do.

Stephens lunged like a snake, brought the club down upon the noggin of Anderson, again and again, until the body keeled over onto the floor, the head a crushed, massy, messy pulp of oozing grue and brains. He then knew it was time for an impromptu exit.

†

The train pulled up to the station, and a bevy of reporters mobbed the thin, ungainly man sitting handcuffed next to his guards.

The man, despite the long, tiring journey he had undertaken, despite the handcuffs and the constant attention of reporters and lawmen who were watching him like the proverbial hawk, was more than eager to speak of his strange, sordid catalog of sins.

"When did you first think of killing them?" one of his interrogators asked, genuinely intrigued by the manacled monster before him.

To which Mr. Richards replied:

> Eight or nine days before I did it. I had selected my companion for life, and I expected to bring her to this farm, for a while, at least. I saw that the arrangement was not going to be satisfactory, and considering the source of life, and its end, it struck me that it would be just as well for everybody if the whole family were out of the world. I thought the matter over, thought of the best way of disposing of the bodies, the chance of discovery, and made up my mind the scheme was a good one.
>
> If I was discovered to this, so I was liable to be discovered in the old matters, if I didn't do it. The neighbors all thought she was going to leave the country, and wouldn't know but she had gone as she expected.
>
> We were up all night Thursday, October 31st, making preparations to go, Mrs. Harelson making clothes for the children and getting them ready. I was to take them to Hastings, where they were going to take the train. We were up nearly all night Friday night, and Saturday night until 3 or 4 o'clock Sunday morning. I had decided to dig a place for their remains as close to the straw stack as I could get, and watched for a chance to prepare it.
>
> I expected them to use the straw from that side and scatter it over the spot. I had a watch, but it was not running, so we had no time piece, but it was between 3 and 4 o'clock when I went out to feed the mules. Then I took the shovel, a common railroad shovel, and commenced digging the hole. I am pretty handy with a shovel, and in half an hour I had a hole about 2 by 6 and three or four feet deep. It was in a place that had been

ploughed for three crops. I had agreed, when Mrs. Harelson went to bed, to call her at half past 5 or 6.

I had everything ready to get a warm breakfast in five minutes, the grain was loaded and I was all ready to start for Hastings. I went into the house, found them all sleeping soundly, got the axe, and went at the job.

The statement that I dashed the baby's brains out on the floor, breaking one leg is not true. I killed them all as they were sleeping. Mrs. Harelson and the two oldest girls were in the bed together and the baby in the crib. I killed Mrs. Harelson first, then the second child, then the oldest one, and the baby last. There wasn't one woke and there was not a sound made. I only got blood on one blanket and on the pillow shams. This bedding I took out with the bodies and threw into the hole. I carried Mrs. Harelson's body out first, then the two girls at one trip and took the baby last.

If the baby's leg was broken by me it was when I threw it into the hole. I picked it up, carried it out and threw it in as I would a log. I hauled in the dirt without being particular to put the yellow under dirt at the bottom, where it had come from. I presume that led to the discovery of the bodies when the neighbors were searching. I examined the house carefully, found I had left no spots of blood anywhere and that the ax was clean.

If any hair was found on a flat iron it was not human hair. I then straightened things up and cooked and ate my breakfast . . .

Mr. Richards went to the gallows quite willingly, with nary a complaint as to his punishment. Which, all things considered, he seemed to think of as rather just.

He was executed January 15, 1879.

CHAPTER 18

Unsolved and Unnerving

The Haunted History of the Vilisca Axe Murders

The world of Victorian murder is one popularized by the legend and legacy of men and women like the pseudonymous Jack the Ripper, Dr. H. H. Holmes, Dr. Thomas Neill Creme, and Lizzie Borden just to name a few. The blood-soaked saga of the Moore family of Vilisca, Iowa, dispatched unceremoniously from this world by an assailant who was never apprehended, is a case that altogether has, most likely, missed the attention of even most serious crime buffs. Yet, it is a case that resonates down to this very age, when television and Internet celebrity would have pushed the sensational details through the increasingly vapid and short-attentioned intellect of the common prole.

Today, bored housewives, unemployed schizophrenics, and those who are religiously glued to TruTV could savor the sickening saga, sip the sordid soup, imbibe the bloody details to their sadistic, vicarious thrill-seeking black little hearts' content. And they did quite the same in 1912, too, although on not such a grand scale. (And not through an electronic media apparatus, of course.)

The details are simple.

A few recreations, in much the spirit of the late, great Leonard Nimoy's old television program *In Search Of*.

†

The two young girls were giddy at the prospect of spending the night with their friend.

"Oh, Dolly!" said the one. "It will be ever so much fun! We'll play as if we're great ladies, over for a very serious, capital tea!"

"Yes," agreed the little Moore girl, who took some umbrage at being called Dolly, but, nonetheless, was just as eager to drink from toy teacups at their own Mad Hatter's Tea Party as Ina Mae and Lena. "But do remember, we must attend church first. Mother has worked ever so hard on the children's service, and we shan't miss it."

(I have no record, of course, indicating that the girls spoke like charm school princesses. However, not being much in the way of what young girls were like a century ago, I am dictating directly from the macabre little ghosts in my head.)

Ina Mae and Lena Stillinger were over for the night. It would be, unfortunately for them, the final night of their young, tragic lives, cut brutally short by the hands of an unknown perpetrator. Perhaps as the sun began to dip behind the trees, they reflected, for a moment, on the brevity of life upon this earth. Most likely, they thought nothing at all.

Sometime that night, while the world was shrouded in blackness, he or they came into the home, gaining access in some mysterious way. They proceeded up the stairs to the master bedroom. It was here that they found the parents sleeping soundly (we must assume), inured against the perils of the world. It was then that he or they raised an axe, and, in a cold and savage and brutal act of murder, snuffed out their very lives as they lie in bed.

Next, they went into the children's room, and . . . took care of them. The scene must have been one of outright, brutal and bloody atrocity. The bodies were very quickly piling up. What, pray tell, could possibly have been the motive for this massacre?

Downstairs, the two luckless young Stillinger girls (who had picked the very wrongest night they possibly could have to stay over for a slumber party), were dispatched. One of them lay across the bed, her arms showing signs that she had struggled to keep the mortal blows from falling on her pretty face. Did they know the identity of their attacker, perhaps? Who and why? (These are two questions, most likely, that will never be solved.)

And then the killer must have slipped out, leaving behind him (presumably a him) cold cadavers congealing in pools of sickening grue.

The final body count ran as follows: Mr. Josiah Moore, his wife Sarah, Herman Montgomery (age 11), Mary Katherine (age 10), Arthur Boyd (age 7), and Paul Vernon (age 5). Additionally, the two Stillinger girls, bringing the mad total to eight human beings. (The unsettling question that keeps echoing in this author's brain is: What could have inspired it?)

The bodies were discovered the next morning by Mary Peckham, a next door neighbor. She had started to worry.

"My, they ain't come out to do their chores! Or even let out the chickens!" (Such, we may imagine, are the simple exclamations of wonderment given to the rural inhabitants of Iowa in 1912.)

Unnerved by this complete disregard for standard operating procedure, Mrs. Peckham launched herself over to the front porch of the Josiah B. Moore residence, pounding stoutly on the door. No answer.

Knock, knock . . .

Still no answer.

She decided that she must call Mr. Moore's brother to come and investigate. What if, for some reason, they had all taken sick and couldn't come to the door? At any rate, she decided, it was all right peculiar. She could get no one to come to her knock.

"Why," she must have said to herself, "the whole place is as quiet as a crypt."

First, though, she stopped to let out those damn chickens.

Brother Moore quickly put in his appearance, and, fearing the worst, had Mrs. Peckham wait out on the porch while he investigated matters inside.

Climbing the steps, he must have felt as if he had stepped into the waiting jaws of some vicious, hungry nightmare.

Blood spattered the walls and dripped out onto the floor; it was the blood of his brother, his sister-in-law, his nieces, and nephews. Did his heart stick in his throat? We don't know. We just. Don't. Know.

The man went to fetch the police, and, soon, a passel of law enforcement officers and others had gathered at the site of the massacre, and a local doctor, peering in through a window (in those bygone days when crime scenes were less controlled than they are now), saw, to his horror, that there were two more lying in pools of their own bright blood . . .

"Oh God, everyone lying dead in their bed!" was, reportedly, his choked response.

Indeed, someone had come in with Hell riding their back, had silently and certainly slinked from room to room, had left a butchers' mess, and had slipped back out, into the night, wild and bloody from his demonic work. (Again, I am assuming, of course, it is a "his." The odds of it having been a woman are slim to none; but, well, stranger things have happened.)

The killer had various, bizarre predilections, according to the anecdotes I've been able to glean:

For starters, he (she? they?) insisted on covering the *mirrors* in the house with black cloth. Why, has never been ascertained. Melodramatic people will claim it was so that the Monster could not see his own monstrousness, and be accursed by it. (In this case they may be right. Interestingly, a weird variation on this theme appears in the book and film of Red Dragon by Thomas Harris, in which the killer, Francis Dolarhyde, leaves bits of broken mirrors in the scooped-out eye sockets of his victims.) Others may conjecture various and sundry explanations, but they all must, inevitably, range around the psychological aberrance of the killer, his obsessions and abnormalities. Further confirmation, perhaps, of "coded" signals within the crime scene tableaux include the fact that a side of bacon (?) was left on the floor in the room where the nearly-decapitated bodies of the Stillinger girls were left to dry in pools of their own blood.

The killer had taken time, after his grotesque work, to stop and eat; why he carried a chunk of bacon with him, why he dropped it on the floor (accident? red herring?) can only be a matter of conjecture. Was he leaving a taunting clue? Is the bacon (pig) a metaphor (hog) for the people he so detested he stepped into their lives and ended them (slaughtering the hogs)?

Bacon. We don't know why. But leave bacon on the floor, he did.

Of course, nothing remotely like this had happened in Vilisca, Iowa; at least, not within recent memory. The outcry and reverberations, though, were felt clear across the United States,which heretofore had been obsessing over the tragedy that had transpired in the North Atlantic when a particular legendary ocean liner ran into a fatal iceberg on her maiden voyage, carrying John Jacob Astor, W. T. Stead, and other prominent men of their era to a watery grave. (But *not*, of course, the "Unsinkable" Molly Brown; whose name, incidentally, was not actually "Molly Brown.")

It is hard to believe that the era of Chaplin, Mack Sennett, the Keystone Cops, and too many other great silent film memories could *still* be so primitively Victorian, but, so it was. There was no CSI lab, no DNA, no scientific analysis available, no electronic trail, Internet, or even a silent film director hiding in the bushes in time to yell "Cut!" and command the crew to wipe up the stage blood. Crime scene investigation had *not* substantially progressed much from the time when Jack the Ripper was carving the vulvas out of drunken hookers in the slums of East London.

Hence, no perpetrator was ever apprehended; at least not satisfactorily, in this world. But, this is the dispensation of the (earthly) side of this horrendous, baffling mass murder. This, as they say, is how the shit went down.

†

Suspects

Andrew Sawyer

The vagrant walked into the railroad camp, looking for a job. Maybe he hadn't eaten in a few days; he looked as if he had slept in his clothes and smelled as if he needed some contact with soap and water.

The foreman, a Mr. Dyer, saw fit to give the snazzy transient a job "on the spot," as it were. Mr. Andrew Sawyer dug in with both hands and went right to work—his only distraction seeming to be his axe (which he curiously slept with) and a newspaper account of the Vilisca *axe* murders, which he secreted away and read with painstaking care. By himself. Alone.

(And his aloofness and aloneness did so bother the other railroad workers that they complained about it. Also, that he slept in his clothes, which was probably another way of saying his hygiene did not meet even their own admittedly loose standards.)

He later elaborated on various theories concerning the crime. Also, according to at least one eyewitness, he suddenly, when approached from behind, reared up his head and said, "You goddamned sonsofbitches, I'll cut your heads off!" He then began swinging his iron and wood bedmate to and fro, no doubt scaring the hell out of everyone within fifteen paces of him.

All of this slowly began to convince the foreman that, perhaps, just perhaps, this Andrew Sawyer might be a likely suspect for the murders that occurred in nearby Vilisca.

But, wait! There was more.

Mr. Sawyer confessed freely that, on the morning the bodies were discovered, he fled Vilisca, fearing to be taken as a possible suspect. He likewise led Mr. Dyer's son, J. R., on an examination of the grounds of the murder house property, describing the way the killer escaped the scene of the atrocity (by stepping from a felled tree, into a creek, first having vaulted a manure box—and maybe swam the bloody English channel, for all we know), and this was confirmed by J. R.'s finding of dried footprints . . . somewhere in the vicinity. It all seems rather vague since 1912, does it not? (Mr. Sawyer, curiously, had mud on his shoes and wet pants when he contracted for the job on the railroad. What had he been doing?)

Hence, Mr. Sawyer soon found himself behind bars. Unfortunately for those who wanted a neat little wrap-up to the case involving a wandering, psychotic transient, Mr. Sawyer had an air-tight alibi: He had been in *jail* in Osceola when the murders were perpetrated, and had been sent home on a train the day the bodies were discovered; as to all the rest of the incriminating behavior, who can say?

Moving right along . . .

"Reverend" George F. Kelly

Classic sexual deviant, or somesuch. Hiding in the convenient frock and dour, large-billed hat of an itinerant minister. Reportedly mad as the proverbial hatter. As a boy, he suffered the sort of bizarre mental breakdown that can only be the incipient onset of syphilis, a history of incestuous abuse, brain fever, catarrh, dropsy, or playing pinochle without properly washing his hands. We jest blackly, of course, but the fact of the matter is: *he was not playing cards with a full deck of 52 . . .* (if you take our meaning).

At any rate, the pathetic perverted pastor plied his trade while, surreptitiously, peeping people—neighbors, their children, etc. Pedofiliac voyeur, we assume. ("Chomo," by prison parlance.)

And, when found out, he got in a spot of trouble for trying to employ women and girls to pose (*ahem*) "in the rough" for him, for a few pictures. (One wonders, given the primitive state of photographic technology, if Polaroid-style instant cameras were even available by 1912? I'll check that later.)

Today, this offense would be enough to *bury* him behind bars, if he were convicted. At the time, he received a slap on the wrist and a few months in a sanitarium. Toddle on off now, Mr. Mentally Deranged.

On June 8, 1912, this unhappy soul found himself teaching Sunday School or somesuch in Vilisca, Iowa. At a congregation meeting, one attended by the eight individuals that would, hours later, be hacked up like cordwood. Why he had come and how he had managed to obtain employment are matters we cannot fully answer. Of course, in an era before computerized records, some men wandered about claiming *anything* about themselves. And it was a damn spot of bother to check the veracity of their claims against the truth of the situation.

On June 10, the ce-divant pastor found himself leaving the Vilisca, Iowa, area while the bodies were not yet cold. In succeeding years he would evince a strong attraction to the case, sending letters to the police detailing:

> I can see it all so clearly! The killer sneaking around the grounds, his shoes covered by strips of fur to keep the dirt from them. He gains entrance, moves, like a panther, down the hall, hefting the terrible enginery of death in both quaking hands! He comes to the children's room. Alas, like twin angels of mourning the little babes lie asleep, arm in arm, in their beds, unaware at the ghastly fate that is to be theirs in the space of a few moments. His heart hammering in his chest, his blood running cold, the dastard heave-ho's the agent of murder, bringing it down, again and again, upon the head of the defenseless girls.
>
> The eldest must have raised her arms to shield her face. Perhaps she placed herself between the path of the axe and the body of her sister, as only a dead, blessed, sweet angel of mercy would under such an appaling and final assault. But it was to no avail, a pointless gesture; the blood

> dripped down from the fatal wound, and pooled across the floor. It was *the shame of the age!*
>
> (Note: Whether or not Rev. Kelly wrote in such melodramatic, purple-prose terms, I—as I was up at three of the clock in the morning, of Christmas Eve 2015—composing this lurid tome, find it to be much in the way of my liking, and so, and so, and so forth . . .)

No doubt, it was his rambling missives to the police, wherein he attested that he could "hear" and had "seen" aspects of the Vilisca murders, that first tickled the nostrils of the police agents—knowing him to be a mental case, they let it go at that. In 1914, he was sent to St. Elizabeth's mental sanitorium in Washington State. In 1917, he was arrested and subjected to a grueling series of interrogations. Twice, he broke, confessing to the killings.

He then recanted. After two trials, he was found not guilty. Whatever his eventual fate, it is unknown to me.

Frank F. Jones

Next on the list of potential killers is Frank F. Jones, a local businessman with a John Deere dealership, who eventually made his way to the state senate. Apparently, Mr. Josiah Moore had been an employee of Jones in the past, before having a falling-out. He left to start his own farm equipment dealership, thereby stealing business away from his former employer. That he was also, reputedly, having an affair with Mr. Jones's daughter is a legendary bit of gossip that was never conclusively established.

Henry Moore

A further suspect, a family slaughterer with a tremendously unappealing mug and jug ears, was thought to have been the culprit. This unappetizing man, Henry Moore, had killed his momma and grandma with an axe . . . and it was believed he liked it so much he repeated the transgression again and again. In other words, he was a serial killer before the world knew what a serial killer even was. Photographs of him suggest a deeply violent character, full of tempestuous menace.

Mr. Moore was born 1871 to a mother who was a nurse and father who served in the Civil War. Several siblings died prior to 1911. Mr. Moore, as noted before, had a distinctly unappealing visage. (What do you expect from an axe murderer?)

After having served eleven years on a forgery charge, Mr. Moore returned from prison to live with Mama and Grandmama. Several months before the Vilisca horror, both women were found bludgeoned by an axe. Mr. Moore confessed during his testimony to having lived with the women for a short time after his incarceration. At the time, a number of axe murder victims had cropped up—in Colorado (the Colorado horror being the murder of the Burnham-Wayne family, a husband and wife bludgeoned to death as they slept), Kansas, and Illinois. Could this all be the work of the demented Mr. Moore? Investigators thought it possible.

Mr. Moore served the great remainder of his ugly, embittered, blood-soaked life behind bars. In 1956, the governor puzzlingly paroled him. Whither went Mr. Moore after this, none can say. (Bringing to mind, for some reason, William S. Burroughs's line from Naked Lunch: "What happens when they walk out and leave the body behind?")

Barring the introduction of further evidence, I must leave Mr. Moore, uglier and uglier in death and memory, as simply a potential suspect, a question mark. At least, as far as *other* axe murders are concerned.

William "Blackie" Mansfield

Bringing us to a perturbed possible multiple murderer who, feeling indignant at the light investigators were shining upon him, sued the authorities . . . and won.

William "Blackie" Mansfield was thought the most likely suspect at one point. A baldish, average sort of fellow, he was what, at that point in history, was commonly referred to as a *cocaine fiend*—one can image those words writ in dripping letters over some old-time silent film starlet, a tragic ingenue whose first role was in a propaganda piece exposing the dangers of jazz music, marijuana, and consorting with black guards, heels, and that veritable incarnation of Satan on Earth—the terrible "Cocaine Fiend!"

Mansfield was believed by a Detective Wilkerson of the Burns Detective Agency (off-brand Pinkertons?) to be the killer of other families using the Vilisca MO: windows covered, faces covered, bloody wash basin, foodstuffs eaten, etc. (Was there bacon on the floor? One wonders.)

Detective Wilkerson believed Mansfield (a.k.a. David Worsley, aka Turnbaugh) was responsible for eighty-sixing his mother-in-law, father-in-law, wife, and infant son in Blue Isle, Illinois, in July of 1916. Also, of victims in places as disparate as Kansas and Colorado. Always the same MO, those striking similarities: covered mirrors, windows, etc.

Fortunately for Mansfield/Worsley/Turnbaugh the "Cocaine Fiend," an employee payroll slip proved conclusively that he *could not* have committed the Vilisca murders.

(What of the others? Isn't it more than likely that it was, indeed, all the work of some vagrant serial killer, some transient skipping around merrily, state to state, lurking in the shadows with his axe, no doubt breathing heavily as he watched old-time haus frauen put wash up on the lines, men sitting out on the porch with their pipes and papers, innocent little babes playing ball and skipping rope, and walking in perfect, angelic repose through the tall grasses and gentle rolls and dips of their own front yards, just before washing up for dinner. Little heads bent over the plates, hands folded in prayer. The scene must have nauseated this lurking basilisk of hate, who was always spying, always waiting for his opportunity to strike.)

Joe Ricks

A man giving the name "Joe Ricks" got off a train on June 15, 1912, with shoes covered in blood. This was in Monmouth, Illinois, and the bizarre condition of the man marked him, immediately, as a suspect.

The sheriff quickly claimed sixteen-year-old Ms. Fay Van Gilder, a young girl (a cousin of Josiah Moore, incidentally) who had, reputedly, been accosted by a man in town the preceding Saturday to the murders—she claimed the man had demanded directions to the Moore house. The next day, of course, everyone was found dead inside.

Mr. Ricks, however, at least according to Miss Van Gilder, was not that man.

"Ricks of the Bloody Shoes" disappears into the murky fabric of history, his fifteen minutes expended.

A Last Suspect

The last suspect, a confession from a prison inmate that came decades later, was likewise simply an insane person's attempt at self-aggrandizement. For whatever purposes, we can only speculate.

†

Axe murders seem to have been endemic during this quaint, pre-WWI period. In Louisiana, a Creole lovely named Clementine Barnabet was convicted of murdering *ten* people with an axe, and a news sheet from the period announces how she confessed gleefully to the atrocity. Not having studied the case at any great length, this is all the information I can offer. (Note: there is much, much more to this 1911 case; apparently Clementine Barnabet was part of a cult that preyed upon fellow blacks, a supposed "voodun" cult. Though it has no place in this book, expect more about this case from this author in the near future.)

Of course, at the tail-end of the last century, Lizzie Borden was said to have taken an axe and given her mother and father variously forty and forty-one whacks. Quite a sizable amount of whacks, I take it, for a spinster Sunday school teacher. At any rate, Lizzie was acquitted.

Her eternal repose, however, is a matter of some conjecture, as the "Lizzie Borden Bed and Breakfast Museum" is thought to be quite a haunted attraction, what with guests claiming spectral shadows and shivering screams, and even ghosts climbing into bed with them. I suppose it all *could* be true; I'd like to think that it most certainly is. However, the Lizzie Borden Bed and Breakfast is in Massachusetts, Fall River, a long way from Vilisca, Iowa.

Of course, just like the creaking old Victorian Borden residence, the Vilisca Axe Murder House is reputedly haunted by the spirits of those eight human beings whose lives were so brutally, cruelly, and bafflingly snuffed out more than a century ago now. Visitors have sworn that they have picked up EVPs, or "electronic voice phenomenon," of children crying, of a man saying: "I killed the kids," etc.

Former tenants (pre-1990s) lived in the house, but were reported to have run screaming from it in the night; claims have been made that shoes left about have been found filled with . . . blood. That they were frequently tipped over on their sides and that clothing was strewn about. Darker, more sinister happenings have been said to occur there, the most gruesome being the shadow figure of a man, standing at the foot of a bed, swinging his axe eternally.

Of course, such a domicile could act as a conduit of energy for something black, something negative and vile, something from the past that refuses to die.

The image of the masked killer covering up the mirrors ("See me, see me, I can't have them see me!" I can imagine as the spooky, whispery voice in his head) and the faces of the dead, eating his lunch, his lust for blood slaked, his physical hunger needing to be sated . . . and then, disappearing into the shadows of history, leaving behind the odoriferous stench of suffering and tragedy, of swirling evil. Was this imprinted on the environment?

Shoes full of blood? Mysterious shadowy figures wielding axes, eternally ready for the big chop-chop? Wailing, ghostly infants, reliving, forever and ever, the agonized final moments of their traumatic, untimely deaths?

Could it not be?

CHAPTER 19

The Tragic End of Teena Brandon

The Killing that Started a Movement

The scene was stark, haunting: The young couple videotaped their surroundings, which seemed oddly frozen forever in a horrific moment of time. I felt as if I were watching the misspent minutes of my own fractured youth, felt as if I could see phantoms from 1993 walking around, living their timeless lives, prisoners of the demon *memory*.

But the only memories here were of poverty, hardship, murder, and betrayal.

This is the house where it happened. This is the house where Teena Brandon was murdered.

I myself didn't hear about the case when it happened. Wasn't aware of it, and would have dismissed it as just another tragic murder, albeit one with a weird quirk of fate as far as the victims were concerned. Perhaps it was just that, another forgotten footnote in the annals of Midwestern white trash America—a subject for a few cheap tabloids, nightly news shows, and a biopic. A penny dreadful occurrence that would soon be forgotten.

But some things can *never* be forgotten. Some drumbeats go on and on; some monsters refuse to die. Ghosts don't go to sleep. They, quite often, walk the boring treadmill of their earthly existences over and over again, flashes of their corporeal lives played out in brief flickers for the sensitive. Time seems to occupy the same space, or vice versa. Perhaps we would make better sense if we just admitted we thought some actions are always imprinted on the environment of where they occur.

It is the same at the Teena Brandon death house. The young couple walked into the deserted place, took some video for You Tube. The house itself had moldered under nineteen (as of this book's printing twenty-two) years of time, hard for me to believe. Whoever has occupied the place in that space of time has left behind the trash and detritus of dissolute living: beer bottles, fast food wrappers, and other filth. But the rooms are eerily empty, echoing—one imagines heavy with must and shut-in age. Heavy with spent grief.

(Perhaps whatever evil swirled, like cold, heartless shadows, around the place, attracting to it the tragic events that later transpired, haunted the successive decades of partiers. Maybe their revels wore thin, a little gruesome—who would rent such a place? Is horror and evil attracted by a particular locale as in a bad novel? Do the tragic, violent events that transpire in such sordid locales linger there, like psychic footprints, like the high, wafting stench of an odious, rotten thing, to be detected by those with sensitivity to such spiritual vapors, even after decades have elapsed?)

One of the most eerie points in the short video comes when the camera focuses in on a single, mildewed bouquet of flowers, set in the center of the room where the murder of Teena Brandon took place—left, like a bird that has fallen from the sky, to mildew, left in memoriam by some unknown hands, some visitor that preceded the video makers. Again: Do certain places gather in tragedy, like a whirlpool of sickness? Can a haunting be retroactive? Can ground be cursed? Or even: Can a human life play out its own curse? Are we the victims of predestination, or do we create our fate, weave the webs of our existence, strand by strand as we go? These are heavy, ponderous questions.

Teena Brandon/Brandon Teena was born in Lincoln, Nebraska, in 1972, the baby of a family that included one sister and a father who would soon die, at age eighteen, in a freak automobile accident. Little Teena and her sister would have been left the children of a single mother, had not mother, JoAnn, decided to marry again. This seemed to be more a matter of convenience than anything else, but, for her girls, this was the most stable period of turbulent, latter-twentieth-century childhoods. They loved and cherished their stepfather, and he them.

Alas, it was not to last. Jo Ann Brandon felt she couldn't live with that man, and, despite their best efforts to "make it work" for the kids's sake, the couple finally called it quits. This must have been traumatic for Teena, who began to develop the confusion over sexual identity that would follow and come to define her for the rest of her short life.

†

We should stop here and get something straight: Teena Brandon was no angel. Matter of fact, contrary to popular portrayal, she was not, I think, entitled to the posthumous sainthood accorded her by Hollywood. But I should explain.

After Teena's mother divorced "Jug," Teena and sister Tammy tried, unsuccessfully as might be imagined, to maintain a relationship with this man, something his new girlfriend was having none of. Eventually, Teena's mother gave him the ultimatum of Jug's new girlfriend, or visitation with the girls. As also might be expected, Jug decided in the favor of "moving on."

Tammy claimed Teena never forgave him for this. The psychological impact of this abandonment, a second father that Teena Brandon failed to be able to connect with, became apparent as the sexually ambiguous young girl began to develop.

As a Catholic schoolgirl at the exclusive Pius X school, Teena became a misfit, a prankster, and class clown, who began to dress in ties and boys' slacks, ran around with girls that dyed their hair purple, and stole toilet seats. Childish pranks, but a forerunner of what was to come, at least for Teena Brandon.

Unable to properly connect with her peers, it was a relief when Teena was finally able to foment a friendship with the youthful Sara, a girl from a rival Catholic school. Both talked at length about their troubled home lives, Sara confiding about her "crazy bitch" of a mother, who was obsessively Catholic, called her daughter a "slut," and had set up a grim altar in the living room that the entire family was expected to genuflect before when entering or leaving.

Teena likewise confided about the sexual abuse she allegedly suffered at the hands of a relative. "Basically Jack," Sara would recount, as an explicit description (which I can only assume means that the relative exposed himself and masturbated in front of Teena).

Soon, a strange, confusing rift began to develop in Teena's personality. A bank book she kept was made out in the name of "Ten-a" Brandon, and she began to take on new, alternate "personalities"; becoming more and more masculine, taking on a personality as "Billy," among other masculine nom de plumes.

Such identities were important, for, soon, Teena Brandon was clowning around rather dangerously with a series of young (underage) girls, pretending to be "Billy," pretending to be male.

It started as a phone prank with a girl named Liz; but after visiting Liz, Teena realized it would be better to hitch up with Liz's young friend Heather, who was fourteen. Teena, to be fair, was only around eighteen at the time, but it was still a dicey relationship. Made all the more so, of course, by the fact that Heather had no idea that her "Billy" was actually a girl.

The relationship with Heather followed what would become a predictable pattern for Brandon: syrupy, sexless lovemaking, gift-giving, a young girl totally infatuated with her new, kind-hearted and sensitive (and undeniably pretty) boy. Brandon was known to ingratiate himself with the mother of such girls, breaking his back doing household chores and seemingly being as helpful as possible.

The dark side of this, of course, was that Brandon was also ripping off Heather's mother by forging stolen checks from her checkbook. It started out as yet another prank: Brandon stole some of the checks and began to buy silly, unnecessary items: CDs, oversized shoes, even writing a check for one million dollars. At the time, she was living with Heather and her mother Ruth (Ruth stood by Brandon even when JoAnn called, panicked at the choices her daughter was making in life, called with undoubtedly troubling information that "Brandon/Billy" was actually "Teena").

Eventually, Heather was apprised of the fact that there was something unusual about her new boyfriend. When confronted by the fact that Brandon was actually born female, Heather was told, by Brandon, that he was actually born a hermaphrodite, that he was seeking sex-reassignment surgery and would soon be fully male. It was all a lie, a story Brandon gleaned from an episode of *Dr. Phil.*

Of course, Brandon was no hermaphrodite, and there was never going to be any surgery. But he deceived one young girl after another with this story, moving from Heather to Reanna, after Heather decided being with a woman impersonating a man was not something she could easily cope with.

The same situation played itself out again with Reanna, who, likewise bamboozled, finally found herself casting Brandon, regretfully, out of her life. Regretfully because he was, after all, so very sweet, gentle, and good to her.

Brandon next set his sights on Gina, a young lady in which he had a hopeless fantasy of romance and living "happily ever after" (the theme of living in a fantasy world, of imagined wealth, beauty, and romance, was one that marked Teena Brandon's entire life. He used to spin endless stories, it is told, of rich relatives, planned trips to Europe, and purchasing hot cars. The reality, sadly, was sordid and impoverished).

Gina was the one, Brandon was certain. After Heather had rather unceremoniously dumped him, he had gone into a tailspin of depression, the likes of which nearly killed him—taking an entire bottle of antibiotics in a halfhearted suicide attempt/cry for help that led to a short stay in a mental health facility. Here, Brandon was pronounced as suffering from transsexualism and a personality disorder. The bitter stress of living with this, coupled with his legal woes (Brandon admitted to having pending forgery charges and possible charges related to solicitation of a minor) had conspired to send him over the edge.

Brandon reportedly, ironically, detested lesbians; his sister Tammy, who suffered, like Brandon, at the hands of abusive lovers (Brandon had been involved in a short pseudo-lesbian relationship as a woman with someone who beat her), had given her baby up for adoption to a lesbian couple, which hurt Teena Brandon very badly. So perhaps his attempt to become male was a psychological mechanism to divert the pain of admitting that she, as Teena, was indeed, also a lesbian. (But I am no psychologist and just speculating . . .)

To try and make sense of Brandon's romantic life requires more effort than what I am willing to expend on it—and it isn't necessary. We can sum it up thusly: Brandon met several, seemingly always underaged girls. She (as he) fed the girls a line, usually revolving around him getting the sex-reassignemnt surgery that would cure his hermaphroditism . . . which did not exist. (Teena Brandon was born fully female.) JoAnn Brandon would step in and try to intervene, but was rebuffed by the delusional young girl, her mother, and Brandon himself. Brandon would "couch surf," bounce around from residence to residence, job to job . . . and steal checks, engage in theft and fraud, get busted for underage consumption, etc. Racking up legal charges, and turning friends into enemies, Brandon was bringing *a lot* of bad karma down on his own head.

His short-lived courtship with Gina Bartu results in one photo of Brandon that is classic. Brandon, dressed in a tux, explodes through the door of a rented hotel suite with the rather large girl held in his arms . . . carrying her "over the threshold." Brandon is obviously straining to just keep the girl's big body aloft. The resultant engagement party consisted of a hot tub filled with beer, much food and pizza delivered, and Brandon getting down on one knee and offering Bartu a diamond ring, proposing marriage. Bartu did not know it at the time, but the entire affair had been paid for by Brandon with Gina's stolen credit card.

†

Brandon was living the go-nowhere life of a slacker. Worse, he was racking up criminal charges and ripping off friends, many of whom wanted to kick his ass for stealing from them. Living with male friends in a trailer park, Brandon soon descended into a situation where he was struggling by as a Kirby vacuum cleaner salesman, impersonating a male with female friends, and spending lavishly on girls who were doing little more than using him for gifts. It was an ugly period for a nineteen-year-old whose life had run off the rails even before it began. Maybe, thought Brandon, it was time to pick up stakes and move on.

To Humboldt, Nebraska. To a final destiny.

†

The two thugs were both drunk out of their minds. They hammered on the door, but that was getting them nowhere. Tom said to John, "You better watch out. Someone in there might have a bigger gun than yours."

John Lotter was past the point of caring. His blood was hammering in his skull, and his erratic, criminal instincts were primed to a razor-sharp point. Alternately, these two Cro-Magnons were just "stuck on stupid," in a homicidal, sickening way. They had to cover their asses; rape, after all, was rape, and they conceived of getting taken down for decades for what they had done just a few nights before.

The door gave with a crack of wood. Inside, the two soon-to-be killers went into the back bedroom. There was a baby, a water bed, and Lisa Lambert, begging them not to hurt her. Kill her. Or her baby.

"Where's Brandon?" Tom Nissan yelled. Underneath the covering of the water bed, he could see feet, movement. It was Brandon.

"No, Tom! No, please! I'm begging you not to do this!"

John Lotter stepped into the room, fired. Brandon crawled to the edge of the water bed, died. Lotter didn't feel this would be sufficient to finish him off, so stepped forward with a knife and stabbed him. That did it.

The water bed was punctured. Blood and water began to leak out, mixing into a sickening, noxious soup on the floor.

"Please, please don't hurt my baby!" Lisa implored them. They didn't. But they killed Lisa, leaving the baby to wail in its crib.

Next came Lisa's friend, Philip Devine, a black man missing a leg. Phillip had been hiding in a closet when John grabbed him, dragging him out. He nearly collapsed in the doorway of the bedroom, looking at the victims on the bed, dying and dead in their respective pools of gushing blood.

"Hey man! You don't have to do this! I won't tell anyone man, I swear!"

"Shut up, n-gger! Sit your ass down!"

John threw Philip Devine onto the love seat in the living room. Mr. Devine had come to Humboldt to represent the Job Corps. The young man had already had a hard, harrowing life: not expected to live after birth, he was considered mentally and physically disabled, was trying to pick himself up from his disadvantaged early beginnings. But, that would all end in one insane moment, this night.

Lotter shot Philip Devine in the chest. The young black man reared back, kicking up his leg, overturning the coffee able, which fell over partially on him.

The two drunken idiots, now mass murderers, must have tried to clean up as best as they could. How effective they could have been under the circumstances, and with the obviously limited IQs they had to work with, can only be a matter of conjecture. Then they left, screeching out of the dirt drive and down the highway, leaving their car tracks for forensic analysts to take note of later.

Also, footprints. Bloody prints. Enough evidence to send at least one of them to death row.

They drove back to town, stopping first to drop a bundle with the bloody knife into the river. Back home. Tom's wife was dragged from her slumber by his insistent knocking. Getting up, she let him in, noting how drunk and panicked he seemed. John Lotter was with him. Tom did a curious thing, having his wife rinse his hands off in bleach, wash his clothing . . . and swear that he had been home during the time they had actually been out. Kandi, the wife, who was notorious, incidentally, for her slovenly housekeeping (actually, more like living in literal filth), was unaware of what had just transpired, but she promised both of them that she would comply. After all, she didn't want Tom Nissan going back to prison (he had already served time for arson).

†

Tom Nissan and his pathetic life is an entirely different can of worms.

Born to a teenage mother, he was adopted by the undeniably disturbed Ed Nissan, who eventually left his young wife when she became physically unattractive to him. He took the kids with him, basically kidnapping them from under her nose . . . she came home one day to discover everyone gone.

She decided to move on with life.

A fuller description might be rendered. Ed, a rather pathetic cabinetmaker, had married Sharon, a fourteen-year-old girl with a baby boy and no prospects, from Rulo, Nebraska. Ed, liking what he saw, decided to snap her up—he was nineteen at the time. Heading out to the JOP, the two were hitched up post-haste, and then Ed took his child bride and her son to Seattle to live. There, Sharon proved to be incurably unhappy, and gave birth to a second child, a stillborn. Which psychologically wiped the floor with her. She decided to head back home, even though Big (I presume) Ed adopted little Scott as his very own.

Back home, they picked up roots to move to Falls City, wherein Sharon decided that she must get pregnant again [she had given birth to a girl for Ed, Susan], and Ed was not happy about this. The journeyman cabinetmaker liked things just the way they were, was unthrilled at the prospect of having another mouth to feed . . . besides, the last pregnancy had stretched his little young honey way out of shape physically, and made her grumpy and irritable . . . no, no. No more kids, Ed decided.

Sharon got pregnant, went into labor on October 22, 1972. (The date of the 22nd *might* have some significance for the esoterically-inclined reader: After all 22 is essentially just 11 + 11. Or, 11/11. But I digress.) And Ed was so involved in his sumptuous dinner that he told her to go to the hospital and have the damn baby all by her lonesome. Which, incidentally, she did.

(Springing from such a warm environment, then, it is little wonder that Thomas Marvin Nissan grew up to be such an undeniable asset to society. End sarcasm.)

Thomas Marvin Nissen (a.k.a Marvin Thomas Nissan) came into the world, unfortunately, kicking and screaming on October 22, 1972, a curse to himself and to society. The doomed toddler was unusual and marked by the behavior during even his first few years: He refused to eat meat, was quiet, strange, and aloof, would often stare into space . . . Was he already having visions of his own grim fate? Are all things, then, predestined to be? Who knows?

The boy grew to not like his parents, particularly his stepmother, with whom he was rarely on speaking terms, and could rarely even be in the same room with. Ed Nissan, who by now had taken the children and left, nonetheless enjoyed calling up the long-suffering Sharon and tormenting her with insane rants and demands, telling her the kids were sick, that he didn't know what to do, that it was her fault if one of them died.

"I couldn't call the authorities because they were his kids, too," she protested lamely, although one wonders what sort of decision a judge would make in that regard. Suffice it to say, little Thomas Marvin Nissan, who would sit on the can for an hour, then, when told to get up, would politely piss all over the floor, during the terrible transition to adolescence discovered the joys of alcohol, marijuana, and hard rock (music).

Disappearing into his room in his new "home" in Eugene, Oregon (after previously living in Memphis, and Falls City, Nebraska), Thomas Nissan is described as disappearing into the world of pot and heavy metal . . . like many rebellious teens from otherwise good homes. But Thomas Marvin Nissan was *not*, most definitely, from a good home. Sharon describes how Ed always hit their son, Scott, with a belt when he was disobedient. Thomas Marvin is described as having just been "slow," but somehow you "just wanted to beat him." (Make of that whatever thou wilt.)

Scott, the older brother, absconded to live with Sharon, eventually—his real momma. Sharon, by that time, had met Bob Popejoy, a man with quite a lengthy criminal record, from a notorious Falls City family that reportedly had their own file at the county courthouse. Not exactly going to win any "Upstanding Citizens Awards," in other words.

And Mr. Popejoy allegedly beat the hell out of Sharon, mother of Thomas (according, at least, to Thomas).

By this point, Thomas Marvin was pretty well confirmed in his alcoholism and profligacy, having taken to drinking and indulging in acts as varied as stealing cars, trucks, running away from home, and generally behaving like the living representative of incorrigible, wayward youth. An unfortunately fruitless suicide attempt left him with a gunshot wound permanently embedded in his chest. "I never could do anything right," he bemoaned from his prison cell while serving his life sentence for triple slaying. I tend to agree.

Thomas Marvin eventually went to live with Momma Sharon and Daddy Popejoy. Mr. Popejoy, the putative stepsire, tried, it is said, in vain to make the boy feel "welcome" (whatever the hell that means under such circumstances) but kept running aground. Thomas Marvin decided he hated him. He must have damn well hated Sharon, too, ("I saw my mom go around with one side of her face purple," he said. Presumably, this was from where Bob Popejoy beat her. She, likewise, was said to have been beaten so badly on one occasion she could not leave her bed for two weeks. One wonders why the authorities were, seemingly, never ever called in on any of this) because he plotted an early murder, perhaps—a foretaste of what, for Thomas Marvin Nissan, was yet to come.

The house had reeked of a flammable material. A trail of suchlike material and doused rags, were found in Marvin Thomas Nissan's bedroom. This was probably the last straw, but Bob Popejoy spared not an ounce of energy in beating the budding arsonist into a sopping puddle of blood. Ironically, Thomas Marvin would later go to prison for an arson he completed.

Other notable instances of sourness in an already meaningless, wasted existence include: the theft of a trucker's rig, the absconding with said vehicle to a different state, stays in youth psychiatric and rehab facilitates, going AWOL after joining the army . . . Need I say more?

I could elaborate with more interesting tidbits in this short, sorry life, but, suffice it to say, since this is not the biography of that renowned humanitarian philanthropist and polymath Thomas Marvin Nissan, I think, at this point, you rather get the point.

After his parole, Mr. Nissan, unfortunately for all, made his way home to Falls City. Here, he chummed and hobnobbed around with that other upstanding pillar of the community, John Lotter. The scene was set.

†

Teena Brandon, as "Brandon," had started romancing a girl named Lana Tisdell, a sort of vacant, rather homely blonde, of a variety I am intimately familiar with as having sprung from the corn-fed loins of Midwestern pulchritude. The genetic stock bespeaks "farmer's daughter"; perhaps, less eloquently put, her family tree descends from the traditional "white trash" that made its way West like something out of a Steinbeck novel, settling in rural communities and bringing with them a personal, largely unlauded trail of hopes and tears. I surely digress here, and have probably offended one or two, but since we hail from a similar background, we feel we have a right to say these things. At any rate, one wouldn't be remiss in depicting her pouring coffee at a truck stop, with great tired eyes and a coif of perfect blonde hair pulled into a ponytail at the back.

She had previously dated John Lotter, whom everyone already assumed was headed for death row, as he was a habitual criminal, and largely incorrigible, and always somewhat frightening, and frequently drunk, and looked like a typical metal head from 1993.

Chase to the cut . . .

It was a Christmas Eve party, December 24, 1993. It was Thomas Marvin Nissan's house—which, predictably, was as filthy as ever. It was a motley assemblage of people, including Nissan, John Lotter, Brandon, Lana Tisdell, Leslie Tisdell, her boyfriend Phillip DeVine, Lotter's girlfriend Rhonda, Mrs. Kandi Nissan, a few odds and ends, lowlifes, and toughs (one of whom was described later as a skinhead or White Nationalist-type, although it is not said he had any problem with the black Phillip Devine, who was dating the white Leslie Tisdell), and children running around in presumably shitty diapers, in the smoke and filth. Or maybe I'm just trying to set the scene.

A rousing Christmas Eve drinking game was taking place while it was steadily snowing outside. Everyone was getting merrily sloshed. Lotter and Nissen, who by now had heard from Lana Tisdell that "Brandon" was really Teena (she had learned this visiting Brandon in jail; nonetheless, she was described as still being "all over him" at the party) were both becoming increasingly drunk and obnoxious, riding Brandon continually about finally "fessing up."

Lotter would later describe to investigators a scene, alternately comic, tragic, and grotesque, in which, allegedly, he forced Brandon out into the Nissen garage, demanded to see proof he had a penis, and was then treated by Brandon to a view of the end of a belt owned by Thomas Nissen. Nonetheless, Lotter bizarrely confessed he attempted or at least wanted to touch it (!), a proposition Brandon understandably recoiled against.

At some point in the night, the wildly drunk Marvin Thomas Nissen began to really berate Brandon, and the two got into fisticuffs in the bathroom, at one point Brandon managing to shove the larger Nissen into the sink.

This enraged the drunken career criminal, who then walloped Brandon, knocking him into the bathtub.

Eyewitness accounts conflict. Lotter's testimony seemed to be largely self-exculpatory. Was Lana Tisdell there at that point? Several comers and goers, including the alleged neo-Nazi, came to the bathroom door, urging Brandon to drop his drawers and prove he had a dick.

> (Or, at least, that he had had the sex-reassignment surgery he told his girlfriends, falsely, he was always in the process of completing. Lana Tisdell later swore she saw Brandon pissing standing up, and believed he/she managed this with use of a catheter . . . because, of course, of his "surgery." She believed he had a surgically-created penis that was simply occluded, or small. Note: This is probably not a book for the little ones.)

At some point, the two drunken monsters (to call them "ogres" would be an insult to ogres), made the decision *for* Brandon; thus, they started the dynamo or engine of mayhem, murder, and violation that would engulf their lives.

So. "Brandon" was really "Teena."

As the humiliated Teena Brandon stood there, Lotter and Nissen realized, once and for all, that they had been duped. Hornswaggled. That their little, oddly-feminine drinking buddy was actually . . . a chick. Well, that was not cool. That was a violation of the sacred bonds of Midwestern white redneck "dudethink." There was going to be hell to pay.

First off, they hightailed it over to nearby Lana Tisdell's house, and informed her (at the ungodly hour of past two in the morning) that her boyfriend was *not* "sex reassigned"—was, in fact, simply a male impersonator.

Livid, she said that she was through with Brandon. Lana Tisdell piped up to inform all and sundry that, from this point on, Brandon would no longer be welcome in their house. (Brandon was actually staying with Nissen, who had bailed him out of jail.) Leslie Tisdell furthermore informed the assembled that she was through dating Philip DeVine; she had no more feelings left for him.

Lotter and Nissen left, still drunk. They returned to Nissen's home. They had to "talk" a few things over with Brandon/Teena.

†

Brandon Teena was forced into Lotter's piece-of-shit car, essentially kidnapped. A few years earlier, the movie Blue Velvet, a sort of surrealistic examination of the "underbelly" of Middle America, had featured a similar kidnapping/"joyride." I have no way of knowing if Brandon ever saw Blue Velvet, but for some reason, the ride that Frank Booth (Dennis Hopper) gives to Jeffrey Beaumont (Kyle McLachlan) seems an eerie cinematic mirror-image. But that film had come out seven years before.

Brandon later testified that he had no idea what roads they traveled down. They were far out into the Nebraska countryside, moving down rutted farm roads and kicking up dust and gravel. Lotter was quite drunk and weaving. At one point, he drunkenly managed to drive into a ditch.

This was very much not good. The terrified Brandon helped Lotter scout around for blocks of wood and large stones to put under the tires; maybe, they figured, they could find something to give the tires some purchase, and they could drive out of the ditch.

Meanwhile, Nissen walked to a local farm and woke up an irate but otherwise friendly farmer, who proceeded to fire up his truck with attached chain and vehicle pulley . . . What are the odds of finding such a helpful, interested Good Samaritan at past three in the morning on December 25th? Miracles, it seem, never cease.

Lotter held Brandon's head down in the V of his crotch. He had to hide him from the glaring lights of the old farmer's truck. Brandon must have realized at this point that he was being held, literally, hostage.

Earlier, they had stopped at a hotel, and Brandon had run up to a phone booth to place a call back to Humboldt, to Lisa Lambert presumably, to beg someone to drive over and get him. Nissen came out of the hotel with his cigarettes. "No one is coming to get you, Brandon. You're not going anywhere, and you know it. Get in!"

Now, free at last from the ditch, Lotter pulled the car up beside what Brandon believed to be an elementary school. Oddly, in an almost nightmarish touch, the silent, dead playground equipment gave mute testimony as to what would happen next. There is, we believe, almost something tragically fitting about this locale.

Brandon was told to take off his shoes. His pants.

"Why, what are you going to do?"

But he had already figured it out.

Nissen told Brandon that he could fight, but, "We'll beat the shit out of you, and it's no use. Because it's going to happen anyway." He took some of his children's toys out of the backseat to make room.

And then he raped Brandon.

She complained that it hurt. It must have hurt very badly. Both physically, and psychologically. Spiritually.

Once Nissen had descended down the sliding chute of human ugliness sufficient to damn him, he got up from the backseat, and gave John Lotter *his* turn. Lotter, it was said later, had needed *two* condoms, because of his incipient sexual dysfunction.

Then they drove off. They told Brandon that no one would "ever know about this. Nothing happened." Furthermore, they told her, quite plainly, that they would kill her if she turned them in.

Returning to the so-happy Nissan home, Brandon was told to go take a shower, so as to wash off any incriminating evidence (blood, semen) that might be used against the two rapists at a later date. Instead, Teena Brandon took the first of a series of steps that should have brought her some measure of justice; instead, as fate conspired, these actions sealed her doom.

She turned up the shower, but instead of submersing herself beneath the spray, she broke out a window in the bathroom, and escaped . . .

He ran to the first place she could go: Lana Tisdell's house. He burst in, presumably awaking everyone inside. Informing them of what had happened, he was taken to the hospital, where curious doctors that had heard, through local rumor, about a young woman masquerading as a man, examined her and performed a rape kit. Brandon was quite clearly traumatized at this point, and recoiled at the idea that he had to disrobe for the examination.

†

The following is a transcript of a tape recording made by Richardson County Sheriff Laux while interrogating Teena Brandon, hours after the rape. Upon reading this material, you will understand why this particular gross, offensive interrogation has been referred to as a "second rape."

(**SL and L**=Sheriff Laux; **B**=Brandon)

SL: After he pulled your pants down and seen you was a girl, what did he do? Did he fondle you any?

B: No.

L: He didn't fondle you any, huh. Didn't that kind of amaze you? . . . Doesn't that kind of, ah, get your attention somehow that he would've put his hands in your pants and play with you a little bit? [Y]ou were all half-ass drunk . . . I can't believe that if he pulled your pants down and you are a female that he didn't stick his hand in you or his finger in you.

B: Well, he didn't.

L: I can't believe he didn't.

L: . . .Did he have a hard on when he got back there or what?

B: I don't know. I didn't look.

L: You didn't look. Did he take a little time working it up, or what? Did you work it up for him?

B: No, I didn't.

L: You didn't work it up for him?

B: No.

L: Then you think he had it worked up on his own, or what?

B: I guess so, I don't know.

L: You don't know . . . Did, when he got in the back seat you were already spread out back there ready for him, waiting on him.

B: No, I was sitting up when he got back there.

L: And you had never had sex before?

B: No.

L: How old are you?

B: 21.

L: And if you're 21, you think you'd have, you'd have, trouble getting it in?

L: Why do you run around with girls instead of, ah, guys being you are a girl yourself?

B: Why do I what?

L: Why do you run around with girls instead of guys being you're a girl yourself?

B: I haven't the slightest idea.

L: You haven't the slightest idea? You go around kissing other girls? . . . [T]he girls that don't know about you, thinks [*sic*] you are a guy. Do you kiss them?
B: . . . I have a sexual identity crisis.
L: A what?
B: I have a sexual identity crisis.
L: You want to explain that?
B: I don't know if I can even talk about it . . .

†

The prior excerpt of the taped transcript gives testimony to the disgusting behavior of a supposed law enforcement officer in this case, a violating and degrading example of bigoted, hectoring ignorance. This was so intense during the interview that a deputy actually refused to stay in the room. Later, this man would be sent out to the site of the rape, where he would retrieve evidence such as beer cans, used condoms, and a rolled-up pair of socks that belonged to Brandon. Later, Laux, when speaking with Lana Tisdell's mother, would say, "As far as I am concerned, you can refer to it as "IT." Meaning, of course, the sexually-confused Brandon.

Aphrodite Jones has correctly pointed out that, based on the rape kit taken at the hospital, Sheriff Laux had more than enough evidence to arrest Nissen and Lotter. Brandon, having frantically called his sister, Tammy, had informed her that Nissen and Lotter had threatened to kill him. Tammy, after contacting the sheriff, was told by him, "Mind your own business, I'm doing my job."

Just doing his job . . .

†

Brandon was terrified. He must have, subconsciously, felt the noose tightening around his neck. That New Year's Eve morning, he called his sister from the Humboldt farmhouse. He was hysterical; Tammy could only get him calmed down by talking about what they were watching on television. Maybe it was reruns of *Roseanne*. Seems, for the era, somehow appropriate.

It would be the last time Tammy would ever speak to her sister. Mother JoAnn Brandon spoke to her a day or so before, when Brandon told her he would be home soon, and "everything would be fine."

Everything would not be fine.

Everything would be pretty fucking far from fine, for young Brandon.

†

Lisa Lambert's mother must have felt she had wandered into a weird museum of horrors, maybe Madame Tussaud's, upon entering the scene of the Humboldt mass murder.

Silence. Inert, bleeding bodies, captured forever in their moment of death repose. Enter the bedroom, and the floor is sopping with blood and water from the punctured water bed. Her daughter is lying on the bed. She is, quite obviously, gone. Beside her, dead, is another individual shot and mutilated, who doesn't look familiar.

The baby is crying. For a moment, the sound seems like an effect on a loop. As if it comes from a stereophonic speaker. But it is a real grandbaby. She goes to pick the starving, terrified toddler up. The killers had decided to leave the child, possibly to die, if someone didn't show up here in time to rescue it. So, Grandma goes and gets the baby, picks him up.

She dials the police. She then goes to the cabinet and retrieves some formula. She feeds the baby. In the midst of death, she preserves life.

The steady drip, drip of blood and time, as she waits . . .

†

I should stop right now and remind you again of one thing: Brandon/Teena was *no* angel. Brandon was guilty of serious crimes, including credit card fraud, forgery, and theft. He had already established a pattern of using and stealing from family and friends, of losing jobs, of reckless sexual behavior, and a total inability to take responsibility for himself and his life. Whatever effect his sexual identity disorder had in all of this can only be surmised by us now, in hindsight. But making Brandon into some sort of saint would be disingenuous.

That said, and no matter how you feel about modern sexual mores, transgenderism, homosexuality, etc., we can *all*, I hope, agree on one thing. *No one* deserves the fate that befell Teena Brandon on December 31.

Lotter and Nissen had dumped a package of a bloody knife, gloves, and a gun in the river. After their arrest (Nissen and Lotter were both brought out onto the lawn of Nissen's home and told to lie, face down, at gunpoint. They were wanted, at this point, for triple murder.), and their wives, friends, etc., began to spill information . . .

I could go into more of this, but I find the aftermath of such an even to be somewhat tiresome. Nissen fingered Lotter for the killer, and Lotter received a death sentence, Nissen received three life terms. In recent years, Nissen has copped to killing the three himself and even written a letter to JoAnn Brandon asking her forgiveness for the unspeakable crime he committed. Lotter has attempted, unsuccessfully, to have his death sentence overturned. Que sera, sera.

Both men are now haggard, wasted shadows of their former selves. In the Aphrodite Jones book *All She Wanted*, a very revealing photo of Nissen and Lotter at the time of their arrests reveals two faces that seem culled from the images of highwaymen out of a medieval woodcut—especially that of Nissen. The viewer could almost begin to believe in reincarnation, karma, the eternal return—the "Wheel of Time," as if both men had been career criminals and cutthroats not only in this life, but in lives and ages previous to this one.

Or, what about ghosts? What about that lonely farmhouse in Humboldt, Nebraska, where, now twenty-two years gone, a shocking night of murder and bloodletting transpired, releasing agony and pain and torrents of tragic grief that must surely, still echo and resound within the walls of the place (assuming it still stands as of this writing, July 5, 2016).

I remember this time as if it were yesterday. I remember flannel shirts, grunge rock, Kurt Cobain, O. J., Roseanne, piercings, the "Year Punk Broke," and the advent of the LGBT rights movement. I remember high school, and being young and infatuated. I wonder what ghosts walk through the shadow land of yesteryear, in an empty house, a scene of murder?

The camera in the YouTube video pans into the bedroom, where Brandon was murdered. Silently, it zooms down on a withered bouquet of flowers someone, some anonymous soul, has left in their wake, as a memorial. Brandon died like those flowers, lying on the floor, a crumpled flower that would forever die.

Finally, actress Hillary Swank portrayed Brandon in the 1997 movie Boys Don't Cry. It was a critically-acclaimed performance.

RIP, Brandon.

CHAPTER 20

A Circle of Snakes

The Mystifying and Revolting Crime of the Grunke Brothers

(Note: These boys are *not* killers, and no one who reads this chapter should be confused on that salient point. However, they *have* been convicted of a revolting and bizarre crime, one frequently indulged in *by* killers; and, well, because the nature of it so fascinates me, and I feel, for some strange reason, the account *belongs* here, I have decided to include them in this little tome. Call it a "harbinger of our social and cultural decline," or just call it cheap sensationalism—call it whatever thou wilt.)

†

The subject of necrophilia will immediately make most people vomit into their paperback book. It is simply a subject so beyond the pale (no pun) that, simply to discuss it or to be known to be *thinking* about it, makes one immediately suspect. I experienced this firsthand when upon ordering, through interlibrary loan, Dr. Agrrawal's text on the subject, the librarian eyed me, as she handed it over, as if she might conceivably pull back a stump.

I shamefacedly left, and made sure to return the blasphemous tome (Necrophilia: Forensic and Medico-Legal Aspects by Dr. Anil Aggrawal) on time. On the whole, the incident showed me that I was, most definitely, on the right track, as far as the subject matter of another book I am busily working on.

Famous necrophiles include King Herod, Periander, Sir John Pryce, Mad Queen Joan of Castile, Henri Blot, Sergeant Francois Bertrand, Victor Ardisson ("The Vampire of Muy"), Utah grave robber Jean Baptiste; and of course Bundy, Gein, Dahmer, Gacy, et al.

Last, but certainly not least, is the love crime of Carl Von Cosel Tanzler, of Key West, Florida, upon whom I based the novel I wrote—Buried. Carl was most certainly not a killer; just a fanatical lover. When his tubercular paramour Elena De Milagro Hoyos died in 1930, he stole the body and lived with it for a full seven years, patiently reconstructing it, piece by decaying piece, until his private (albeit perverted) shrine was discovered by authorities.

(As Carl was guilty only of robbing a grave, Florida having no specific statute against his peculiar crime, and since the statute of limitations had already expired—he was set free. His notoriety followed him, and he moved from Key West to an undisclosed location, where he lived in poverty with a life-sized reproduction of Elena, and a plaster death mask. The authorities had taken away the body and buried it at an undisclosed location. Before they did this, however, it should be noted that the body was put on display for throngs of curiosity seekers at a Key West mortuary. There, a thousand people filed past the strange remains of Elena De Hoyos before they were consigned to the dirt once more.)

A necrophile, according to Erich Fromm, resides on a continuum at the polar opposite end of all that is healthy, loving, and psychological and spiritually sound: "biophilia," in other words, the love and respect for life. The necrophile, on the other hand, does not grow spiritually or emotionally; does not love or cherish life; is cold, rigid, hierarchical, authoritarian, obsessed with feces and flatulence, decay; is exemplified by fascistic thinking; is iced-in in a spiritual sense; is exemplified, according to Fromm, by men like Hitler, who is the very spiritual apotheosis of a necrophile. Dr. Aggrawal, in his most-excellent text, presents a spectrum of ten "classes" of necrophile, ranging from "necrofiliac fantasizers," to "tactile necrophiles," "fetishistic necrophiles," "homicidal necrophiles," and, Type 10, "exclusive necrophiles" (in other words, people that can *only* achieve a sexual orgasm with a dead body).

In recent decades, beyond the flavor-of-the-month tabloid sensations such as Messeurs Bundy and Dahmer, we have had "romantic necrophiles" such as Karen Greenlee, who, in 1979, was convicted of stealing the body of a young man named John Mecure for sexual purposes. Or, because she felt a confused mixture of fantastical romance and sexual attraction. Or? Who knows.

She was later found in the hearse, OD'd on codeine, with a letter confessing her history as a funeral worker, of molesting the dead bodies of young men whom she was oddly, grotesquely attracted to. "I'm a morgue rat. This is my rat hole, maybe my tomb," she writes. But, she lived.

She was put on probation and ordered to undergo psychiatric counseling. Her crime would have been forgotten, most likely, consigned to the crumbling pages of obscure tabloid rags, if it had not been for an article about her included in maverick publisher Adam Parfrey's seminal collection of underground outrages Apocalypse Culture, published in 1989. (The sequel featured an article about Gothic death and necrophilia aficionado Leila Wendell, who ran, at one time, a "death museum" in New Orleans. Wendell claimed to worship Azrael, the biblical "Angel of Death," who appeared to her in visions as a child.)

Greenlee's case inspired a tiny film called Kissed in 1994, but it has remained obscure. More recent cases of necrophilia include the crime of a disturbed man named Anthony Merino, a hospital morgue attendant who was found by a security guard in flagrante delicto with the corpse of a ninety-one-year-old woman. Further cases include the horrifying double victimization of Karen Range— a crime that will leave many with cynical, bitter feelings about the universe and the often macabre way in which it functions.

Karen was murdered by a door-to-door salesman named David Steffen in Roselawn, Ohio, August of 1982. Mr. Steffen brutally beat and slashed the young woman (who was nineteen when she was killed), and semen was discovered on the body. He was convicted, and currently awaits execution on Ohio's death row.

However, he always denied raping Ms. Range. And, oddly, it was discovered that he was actually being truthful.

Kenneth Douglas, a mortuary attendant, was brought up on drug charges, and a routine test of his DNA was put through a computer (a technological feat not possible in 1982).

Much to the horror of authorities, the only match they could come up with was the semen found in the remains of Karen Range, a body that had lain in the morgue Mr. Douglas had worked at—twenty-six years earlier!

Charged with "gross abuse of a corpse," and held on 700,000 dollars bond, it was later believed that Mr. Douglas might have violated as many as *one hundred* dead bodies. A busy boy, he had been. . .

Bringing us to the 2010 crime of the Brothers Grunke. I cannot vouch for the claim that young people today are little changed from their peers and predecessors of past generations. It is not in me to be other than cynical when it comes to the dissolute habits of modern youth, or the gradual social disintegration plaguing the modern United States. I do not propose to lay the blame on the young people; they are symptomatic of a larger illness, one borne, inevitably from the oft-studied cycle of birth, rise to prominence, and entropic decline registered first by men such as Gibbon and Oswald Spengler. I say they are symptomatic of a wasting societal illness, *not* the illness itself.

The story of the Brothers Grunke is short and ugly and sensational, ready-made for a tabloid centerfold. The brothers themselves, particularly the besotted, necrophilious paramour, looked about what one would expect from overindulged, amoral "emo" kids: prone to fixating on dark comic books, self-mutilation, primitive and saccharine post-punk rock (which projects a melancholiac, "Wertheresque" angst that often fosters in its young listeners suicidal ideation), vapid popular movies and television situation comedies . . . the collective product of our modern, Internet-infused, social media "culture." (I do hope I'm not coming off as unduly harsh.)

Curiously, though all three men—brothers Nicholas and Alexander Grunke and accomplice Dustin Radke—were all twenty years old at the time they perpetrated their act, their mugshots make them look much, much younger (I assumed they were all in their early teens). This may clue the viewer in as to the arrested mentality of these individuals, their failure to grow into fully-formed individuals, their need to batten spiritually and even in a physical, sexual sense upon the dead . . .

The dead in this case was a Miss Laura Tenneson, twenty also, who died in an unfortunate motorbike accident August 6, 2006, and whose picture in the local obituaries caught the attention of Nicholas Grunke, who became aroused and then infatuated with the unattainable object of desire. He decided then that, dead or alive, he *had* to have her.

Thus was hatched a madcap plan, a true "Comedy of Errors"; the two men, enlisting the aid of Radke, departed late that September 2nd to exhume the earthly remains of Miss Tenneson, and to perpetrate a lewd, shameful (most would say unremittingly evil, psychotic, and revolting) sexual act upon her dead body.

That they worked themselves up to actually attempting this should come as little surprise to anyone who has been paying attention the last few years at the burgeoning propensity for youth violence—particularly gun-related homicides and mass-casualty shooting incidents. Youth today seem far, far more likely to cross the line from macabre fantasy to grim reality than their predecessors from a generation ago; and, perhaps, this should really not surprise us very much.

But, for all their straining and struggling as they heatedly went about trying to claim the body of Tenneson, they couldn't, for the life of them, get the cement vault open, and Mr. Radke walked back to the car, either in frustration—or maybe to get a crowbar. Who knows?

It was there that Mr. Radke encountered Mr. Policeman. Mr. Policeman, presumably crossing his concerned arms over his chest (at least, that is how I envision it. Most probably he shined his flashlight.), asked the curious young man, who was dirty with grave soil and sweating profusely, just what the hell he was doing in the cemetery at that hour.

Of course, there was no denying it. They had been caught, *ahem*, "red-handed," so to speak, trying to open that grave. To get that "girl"; the object of amorous attention, given bizarre life in the minds of young people who no doubt learned to objectify and depersonalize women and other objects of sexual fixation from viewing Internet pornography (some of which is centered around the concept of necrofetishistic fantasies, of "sleepy sex" with performers who are drugged, or pretend to be dead). All the better to fuel fantasies of power, for the performers to become, in the mind of the viewer, an erotic companion that *will not* reject them because that companion *can not* reject them. There are men who enact such rituals in brothels, with prostitutes made to look like cadavers; alternately, they are attracted to "sleepy sex" sites on the Internet, with models that are drugged (or, at the very least, pretending to be).

The fantasy must be one of submission, to fuck the inert, yielding body, stripped of any will to resist; to make the "living doll" an object of perfect fantasy in the mind of the necrophiliac paramour.

There is very little else to say in this case. The State of Wisconsin, not having any specific law against necrophilia, failed to meet its burden to be able to punish the young men under the existing statute, leaving one politician to quip that, "in a state that has seen the likes of Ed Gein and Jeffrey Dahmer," that it was, indeed, a little strange that Wisconsin did not have a specific law dealing with sex with the dead. The sentences amounted to a slap on the wrist for the offenders, with the proviso that the eldest Grunke brother must seek psychiatric counseling.

(Also, of course, they must register on the web as sex offenders, a registration that should specify the nature of their offense. One realizes, with a kind of ironic smirk, that "necrophilia" is probably *not* something an employer is really looking for in an applicant. Hence, the best job any of these particular perps will probably be able to land in the future is, ironically, digging graves.)

It should be noted that, in 2010, the Wisconsin Supreme Court ruled that the particular legal statute covering sexual violation of a person without their knowledge or consent *does* in fact, also cover necrophilia. Whatever implication this ruling will have on the future disposition of the particular case of the Grunkes, if any, is unknown to the author. One imagines they are safely in hiding or have changed their names. People, you know, can be awfully cruel.

For, as "lonely hearts" killer Ray Fernandez once said, "What do the public know about love?"

CHAPTER 21

Unrepentant

Henry Brisbon Jr., the I-57 Killer

Henry Brisbon Jr., born in 1956, killed for the first time, as far as anyone knows, in 1973. Henry, at the time, was all of seventeen.

Verily, this last dastardly case study is going to be short. But not sweet.

†

Henry Brisbon Jr. hated. Deeply, profoundly. The whole damn world, I take it. He was riding around on I-57 with three other men on June 3rd of that year of 1973. Forcing a woman off the road, they forced her to strip, commanded her to run for her life, then executed her by shooting her between the legs. One gets the picture, for some reason, of actor Joe Pesci in the movie JFK (1991) intoning to Kevin Costner, "It's fun and games man. *Fun and games!*" But, I digress.

Next, motorists Dorothy Cerny and James Schmidt were forced off the road by the murderous punks. They were forced to lie on the side of the road, then were shot to death by Brisbon. The men beat a retreat, but the

I-57 killings would damn them.

Brisbon received a death sentence, later commuted to life because of a Supreme Court ruling. At Stateville Penitentiary he killed an inmate named Richard Morgan. He was later sentenced to death for *this* killing in 1982.

Still, the psychopathic twenty-something was not *quite* satisfied, leaving the courtroom shouting, "You'll never get me! I'll kill again! You'll see! Then you'll have to have another trial! And I'll do it again."

Well then. We know he walked the walk he talked.

His other notable hits included an attempt on the life of infamous "Killer Clown" serial killer John Wayne Gacy, an attempt made by stabbing him repeatedly with a piece of wire. (He killed Richard Morgan with the sharpened handle of a soup ladle.) An attempt that failed, of course; Gacy died of lethal injection in 1994. Brisbon, described as a walking social hemorrhoid, a "testimonial to the need for the death penalty," continued to appeal his death sentence. So far, as far as I can glean, he has escaped dancing to the executioner's fabled song.

He is currently serving out his monumental sentence of 1,000 years. Over the years, he has repeatedly attacked corrections officers and prison staff, and started his very own riot.

Some folks . . .

CHAPTER 22

The Cryptic Ideogram of Hate

The other night I had a strange dream, wherein I was not myself.

I approached the mailbox slowly. Apparently, I was confined to a prison—or, at the very least, I was on my way to being so confined. I opened my box, retrieving a handful of magazines, catalogs, junk circulars, etc. I think much of this was supposed to be from other "outsider" musicians.

Also, there was a note in there, written in a special code. I plucked it out from the bunch, went into the men's room. Went into a stall.

I could hear the voice of a large, presumably black social worker come floating in on the stale air, as if I was watching myself in a documentary about myself. She claimed they had broken the code of my secret accomplice, long ago. I looked at the scrawled piece of paper in my fingers, realized they may have very well broken the code, but I had no fucking clue as to what the weird psuedo-Arabic scrawl on the paper meant.

But, inside myself, I was terrified. Like an animal trapped, I was going into a cage that very night with fellow inmates that, I knew, would probably torture and kill me. For, you see, in this dream, I was no ordinary inmate.

I was supposed to be Jeffrey Dahmer.

†

I've written about Mr. Dahmer before. I well remember the very first time I ever heard of him. Walking with an aunt as a high school friend came up behind us, pedaling on his too-small bike.

"Hey," he said, his pale features painted dimly in the gathering twilight, "have you guys heard about the guy in Milwaukee with the body parts in his house?"

I looked at my aunt. She looked as astonished as I; but, of course, the first thought on my mind was "Ed Gein."

"Yeah," he said, "it's just hit the news. Some guy they think was eating the bodies or something. Pretty sick, huh?"

I don't remember when we got back that night, but I must have turned on the television and seen the crime scene techs take the refrigerator out of Apt. 213 in Milwaukee. I must have seen the mordant, lean, and inscrutable visage of Dahmer, the unappealing and thoroughly mundane cannibal serial killer who would go on to lend his name to modern infamy. What was behind that bland, clueless expression? Did I wonder? I must have wondered.

The 1990s were a uniquely sick time to be alive.

Columbine, Dahmer, Oklahoma City Bombing, race riots, Marilyn Manson, cultural decay on every front. Violence in schools and mass shootings. Kurt Cobain becoming a nihilistic "hero" to disaffected youth, at least a few of whom joined him in copycat suicides shortly after the Nirvana frontman's body was discovered in his Seattle home.

April 1994, baby. I remember the day.

But, Dahmer, again. Born in Ohio to Fundamentalist Christian parents, neither of whom could manage to tolerate each other or stay married, despite their deep religious faith. Jeffrey must have sensed that something was missing from life from the outset. Somehow there was a code he couldn't crack, a secret message he couldn't decipher. He began to feel it; the cryptocracy of hate.

It must have quashed the warmth inside of himself, this narcissism. Perhaps he wandered around the family property, looking at nature with strange, new eyes. Here a dead animal, taken with decay, would excite his senses. Where did he make the connection between such sights and living, breathing, "feeling" again? When did he start to collect roadkill?

In Jeffrey's increasing private childhood realm, a dead dog's skull went up on a backyard pole, like some grisly totem of primitive, savage headhunters. Or an item from black magic. It was a personalized fetish, both a sentinel and a doorway; it promised a bleak, noxious future of death and decay.

After an unsuccessful attempt at college, Jeffrey, having spent his boyhood years with his eager fingers dipped in dog guts (all the while plying the role of "class clown"), joined the Army. Stationed in West Germany, he drank himself into a dishonorable discharge. Curiously, a series of unsolved serial sex slayings of young men occurred in a close proximity to where Jeffrey was stationed, leaving some to suspect that the budding serial psychopath must have started his strange career while drinking himself out of the service.

Coming back to the states, it was evident that Jeffrey, a pariah to his family and a severe disappointment, I take it, to father Lionel, went to live with his grandmother in Milwaukee, taking with him his slumbering pathological narcissism, his confusion, his burning compulsion to kill . . .ensconced in the basement of his grandmother's homey dwelling, Jeffrey brooded over slick gay fuck mags while nursing the cogitating demoniac that gave fuel to his homicidal fantasies.

†

It was hitchhiker Stephen Hicks who first helped Jeffrey Dahmer decipher his own personal "Ideogram of Hate." Hicks was invited to Jeffrey's basement rooms for beer and weight lifting. Jeffrey must have liked the young stud as he leaned back on the weight bench, his shirt off, a beer in his hands.

"Nice, Stephen, man. Man, you've got great muscle tone, man."

Sip of beer. Stephen Hicks may or may not have, at this point, begun to worry.

"Thanks Jeff. Hey man, I've . . . I've, Jesus! Is it that late? Hey Jeff, man, I've really got to get a move on."

Jeff's face fell, I think. Here it was again, someone whom he liked, someone whom he wanted, was going to leave him now. Was going to disappear, and abandon him . . . just as his parents had done to him as a child.

"I'm sorry, Stephen, I just can't let you do that," Jeffrey may have said, his features fallen. At some point, to prevent Stephen from "doing that," he picked up a bar from a weight bench and viciously beat in his skull. He dismembered the body, buried the pieces on his property. Later, he would, for undisclosed reasons, dig the remains back up and smash the bones to bits.

A decade further in time, 1994. Inmate Christopher Scarver, motivated by the same "secret signals," the same hidden code of hate, the same cryptic message commanding him to kill, would sneak up behind the imprisoned Dahmer and proceed to beat *his* skull in, in much the same way as he had beat in Stephen Hicks's brains. Karma has a deadly sense of humor, does it not?

Jeffrey continued to kill, continued to unwrap and unravel the secrets of life and death. Grandma said the basement room was stinking. Jeffrey was coming and going all hours of the night. His drinking, his all-consuming alcoholism, was becoming more and more noticeable. What to do?

Jeffrey landed his job at the Ambrosia chocolate factory, wherein, like some sort of cannibalistic Oompa-Loompa, he spent his days reproducing little chocolate men. According to his testimony, delivered at trial when he was arrested for drunkenly exposing himself to underage youth, this job was a primary source of pride and accomplishment for him. Whatever the case, it helped to get him off the hook.

He was forced to check in with a probation officer, who would no doubt have been shocked and astounded at the steady stream of young men who would end up disappearing down the grisly rabbit-hole of Apartment 213, wherein Jeffrey was now ensconced as perhaps the only white gay man in the overwhelmingly black and Latino complex. The other tenants must have looked askance at Dahmer as he went in and out like a pale, forlorn ghost, frequently, perhaps, reeking of alcohol. In time, just like Jeffrey's grandma, they would come to complain of other, more severe stenches.

Work, work, work. Jeffrey was quite a busy boy. His co-workers at Ambrosia disliked him as "the sort of employee that could eat lunch alone and stare at the wall for half an hour." In other words, a man of completely internal experiences and landscapes.

At home, he was collecting penises in jars of formaldehyde, photographing the bodies of victims in various states of torture and dismemberment, filling up gallon drums with viscera. Did he masturbate into the glistening viscera in the same way as he did dog guts so many years previously? (The amusing death metal band Macabre, who have an entire concept album based around the Dahmer case, open their recording with a song about Jeffrey's affinity for "Dog Guts.")

The rest of the Dahmer story is well-known, the stuff of tabloid legends. Dahmer was busted for child solicitation charges for drugging and molesting Sounth Sinthasomphone, a Laotian immigrant boy who spoke little English. In a brutally macabre twist of grim fate, his brother, Konerak, would eventually end up being killed by Dahmer after escaping the apartment.

The young boy, who ran drugged and bleeding from 213, was found on the street by two African American girls. In a stunning example of police misconduct, when the officers called to the scene responded, they took the doomed Sinthasomphone *back* to Dahmer's apartment, where the tight-lipped and masterfully deceptive cannibal serial killer convinced police the fourteen-year-old Sinthasomphone was his live-in lover.

Pause.

The moronic and racist police *bought* this story without first checking for the boy's age. On the way back, they were recorded joking about how they had to be "deloused" now.

Pause.

Konerak was unceremoniously dispatched. Jeffrey, we should add, at this point, was still trying to make "zombie slaves" by drilling into the craniums of his victims, pouring in acid . . .

Caustic acid was very important to Dahmer, as it was one method he used to dispose of body parts. Keeping them in a vat, he would wait until they turned into liquid sludge. Then he could merely flush the scum down the toilet. (Much like his British counterpart, serial killer Dennis Nilsen, who is still alive in prison.)

Penises pickled in jars. A head in the fridge. Saucepans full of hearts and grue. Intestines in the freezer. Skulls on the bookshelf. Jeffrey entertained fantasies of building an altar, or a "Temple of Bones" (he made a drawing of said altar); he bolstered his interest in all things dark with the music of Black Sabbath, with horror and documentary death films such as Faces of Death and The Exorcist 3, and explicit gay pornography. This was Jeffrey's world.

He pleaded with the judge at his child solicitation trial to let him off—that he would lose his job, and thereby, be deprived of his one true source of "pride" and responsibility. The judge, like the errant cops that delivered Konerak Sinthasomphone back to Dahmer's apartment, bought the manipulative psychopath's deceptive lies. Jeffrey got off with a slap on the wrist and a referral for psychiatric treatment.

And he kept killing. Eventually, the body count reached a whopping *seventeen* victims. The final victim, a young black man named Tracy Edwards, was invited back to Dahmer's apartment for "a few beers."

The beers were drugged. Mr. Edwards awoke, nude, in handcuffs. Jeffrey, he claimed, was sitting in the living room in a seeming trance, chanting. Overpowering Dahmer, Edwards was able to escape, naked, bleeding; he managed to flag down a passing patrol car.

The police must have looked somewhat askance at a naked, drugged black man in handcuffs with an unbelievable story about a white psychopathic male that had drugged and kidnapped him. However, unlike the officers who had delivered Konerak Sinthasomphone back to an unspeakable fate, these policemen followed Tracy back to Apartment 213.

Jeffrey, bleary, perhaps unshaven and reeking of booze, came to the door. In a state of confusion, he tried to smooth everything over with the officers. This time, however, the bestial killer's luck had finally run its course. The policemen entered (probable cause, I suppose), and, even a cursory examination revealed that something therein was dreadfully wrong.

Jeffrey had put off his complaining neighbors about the overpowering stench; he explained it away as a freezer that had quit working, some beef or something that had gone "bad." This might have mollified them temporarily, and bought him time.

These policemen, however, were not to be put off. Upon entering, the cop noticed the painted human skulls on the bookshelf, the Polaroid pics of nude men in drugged states—naked, mutilated. And that was before they opened up Jeffrey Dahmer's infamous fridge.

A severed head peeped out at them from where food and condiments would, in a normal home, usually be stored.

Jeffrey was wrestled to the ground. The rest is true crime history, legendry; that very day (July 22, 1991) I was walking with an aunt when a young man of mutual acquaintance came riding up on a bicycle.

"Hey, have you heard about the guy they just found had all these body parts in his house?"

(Or, something to that effect.)

†

Jeffrey was one of the first great media circuses of the 1990s, which knew its fair share of them: Eric and Lyle Menendez, Lorena Bobbitt, the LA Riots, Oklahoma City Bombing, Kurt Cobain's suicide, Marilyn Manson, Columbine, and of course, O. J. Simpson—all vied for space in the strained public consciousness of *fear* writ in huge bullhead letters across the brainscape of a reeling nation. (And, of course, there was also Waco, the Heaven's Gate mass cult suicide, the rise of the Militia movement, the cultural raspberry of the Clinton-Lewinsky Affair; the first attack on the then still-existent World Trade Center . . . a precursor for the horror that was to come.)

Jeffrey seemed to exemplify the panicked unwinding of a generation of doom, a country grown increasingly restless, rootless, mired in tabloid atrocity and creeping millennial terrors.

The trial was distinctly anticlimactic, save for the moment one angry woman, the relative of a victim, exploded in court, having to be restrained from attacking Dahmer as he sat stoically at the defense table.

The outcome was a foregone conclusion in a state where the death penalty was not an option. Jeffrey read a prepared statement about these not being "hate crimes," never were "hate crimes" (the fact that they were lust murders mitigated them somewhat in his mind?), and he "quite frankly, wanted only death for myself." Whatever.

He was sentenced to around 900 years. In prison he played tennis, gained weight, gave interviews, found Jesus, and refused the option of protective custody. He really should have rethought this last option.

It was in 1994, the same year that Nirvana frontman Kurt Cobain made tabloid history by offing himself with both barrels of a shotgun, that inmate Christopher Scarver, prompted by "voices" that told him, among other things, that he was both Jesus Christ and fated to snuff the life of Dahmer . . . snuffed out the life of Dahmer.

The irony was that Dahmer's final moments would be spent in that most inauspicious of all human activities: cleaning a toilet. Much like his British counterpart Dennis Nilsen, you see, Jeffrey frequently chose this method for disposing of his victims, flushing the sludgy pink aftermath of a bath in nitric acid down the crapper, with only the gallstones left to dispose of unceremoniously.

(One might note the further irony that Scarver, creeping up behind Dahmer as he scrub-scrubbed the prison commode, chose as his weapon a bar from a weight bench—the same sort of instrument Dahmer had used to dispatch *his* first victim, the luckless hitchhiker Stephen Hicks.)

Up went the weight bar, only to be brought crashing down, again and again, on Dahmer's insensate skull. Blood must have poured from the blunt force impact, the skull shattered, the brain rendered useless. Dahmer collapsed, possibly into the toilet, but we can't be certain.

A move by researchers to preserve Dahmer's brain for study was rebuffed by the father, Lionel, who eventually had his hideous son cremated. The current whereabouts of the brain, we take it, are probably at the bottom of an urn.

†

Another murder of the mid-90s that marked, for me at least, an era or decade, was the murder of a short-lived friend of mine by a sex maniac. This young victim, Jason Tuzinski, was known to me from six months spent in a youth facility in Indianapolis in 1989. I shall never forget the day I walked in the place for the first time, as I was alone.

All was quiet. The hallway was short, and the place was dim and felt like a dungeon. Heavy wooden doors led to dormitory-style rooms on one side of the ward, which was separated by the restrooms and showers, the "Day Room," or lounge, and the nurse's station. On the other side of the ward was the girl's rooms, which were fewer.

The other kids were away at classes, so I wandered down the hall to suddenly hear a young man singing to himself in what was isolation.

He was a skinny, scraggly teenager with a goatee, and he was singing Pink Floyd songs. Something about the Wall, but I was a pretty big fan of this at the time, and so I must have started singing, too. In time, we were both standing there like idiots, singing the same Pink Floyd songs. As dismal as I felt at that moment, I felt maybe there was some hope for friendship.

However, since I am *not* a sentimental person, I am not going to bore you with the details about this, as they are trifling and unimportant. Jason

Tuzinski was a moody, bipolar individual given to angry outbursts, who was, ultimately, somewhat unlikable. I shared a dormitory room with him for six months, so I should know. (The last time I ever saw him was when I returned to the hospital as an outpatient. He was still there. He was standing in that hallway, again alone. Where were the other children now? He gave me a comic book about the Sex Pistols.)

Upon leaving the place in early 1990 (which was a relief, considering that the environment of this particular institution was rapidly declining, as more and more volatile inmates were brought in), I maintained a correspondence with Jason and a few of the other kids by letter. This was long before the era of email.

This didn't last long.

(Ironically, my last missive from Jason Tuzinski included the news that two of our fellow inmates at the institution had died. Children. A teen boy and girl. More echoes from that empty hospital hallway, more shadows from 1989.)

Flash forward to 1994.

I would be graduating from high school next year. In the meantime, I was exercising my intellect by working at McDonalds. One fine day, as I was sitting smoking a cigarette (a habit I gave up five years ago), I was flipping through the channels when I happened upon a news report of a murder.

Depicted was a young couple. It was Jason Tuzinski, and his young wife, Kimberly.

I was actually underwhelmed. Emotionally, I was a very calloused young man; most of my time was spent absorbing the messages of heavy metal bands that glorified, at the least, a kind of stoicism. Had I become so calloused that I had, literally, no reaction to this? Maybe I was simply in shock.

I could gain few details of the murder from the news report. The picture shown was a wedding picture; the long-haired, scraggly Jason was dressed in a tuxedo, his bride Kimberly in a white wedding gown. Apparently, they had met at another youth facility, and both were considered "mentally impaired."

I decided not to tell my mother. How could I make her believe, or even understand it? This was the first time, perhaps, I had ever seen someone I personally knew on television, and it was under circumstances too horrific to contemplate.

As young and stupid as I was, I should have figured that the murder would be reported in the paper, a small piece on the second or third page, since it was not local. I finally broke down and told my mother. I didn't save the clipping; for years I couldn't even remember the name of the suspect, nor did I know the disposition of the case.

Until, that is, the advent of the Internet, nearly eighteen years later. One day, near the most unholy holiday of Walpurgisnacht, as I remember, I took it into my head that I was going to do a little research on the subject of my murdered friend (or acquaintance. Whatever.). I typed in his name. I didn't have deep to dig.

A sight called "Find a Grave" led me straight to information and photos of his grave. While I sat looking at the long-weathered headstone, his voice came echoing down to me through the decades, still singing songs from Pink Floyd the Wall, still in that isolation room in an empty hallway in the long-ago year of 1989. (Right now, my YouTube playlist has switched over to a song by The Ramones. Somehow, as I am writing about ghosts of the past, that seems oddly appropriate.)

I felt the chill of a goose walking over my grave. I ferreted out the few details of the murder of Jason and Kimberly Tuzinski.

Gilmer. Frank Gilmer. That was the perp's name. He had given a "chilling" confession, according to the newspaper report. "They had to die," he was quoted as saying. *Why?* one wonders.

The best I could discern, without paying for a subscription to a news archive site, was that Gilmer, at age sixteen, was arrested for raping a fourteen-year-old girl. A note his parents turned over to authorities seemed to suggest Mr. Gilmer was thinking of killing this girl as well. She escaped him, and Mr. Gilmer was sentenced to twenty years. He was, however, released in February of 1994, after undergoing "psychiatric" treatment while incarcerated.

By November, he was ready to slake his thirst for blood.

Under pretence of inviting Jason on a hunting trip, near the Salt Creek area of Lake Station, Indiana, while the men were gathering wood for a fire, Mr. Gilmer proceeded to smash Jason in the face with an axe. Noting, though, that this did not sufficiently injure him to cause death, he then stood on his neck until Jason was suffocated. Hiding the body in some dense woods, he then proceeded to Part B of his plan. Part B included the rape and murder of Kimberly Tuzinski; perhaps the motive behind the actions Gilmer took that day. (Which, incidentally, must have been on or around November 6th.)

Going back to their mutual place of residence (Gilmer was a "friendly neighbor") at Pine Village mobile home park, Gilmer persuaded a panicked Kimberly Tuzinski into the car, because, he told her, her husband was having some sort of problem, and he needed her immediate assistance. She might have dealt with such a situation before, or, perhaps, in the heat of the moment, she simply could not stop and do the logical thing by calling the police; however, for whatever reason, the fatally naive young woman got in the car with Gilmer and was driven to the same remote area . . . and to her doom.

Gilmer strangled Kimberly Tuzinski, standing on her neck, as before with Jason, to break it. Not thinking this sufficient to end her life, he dipped her head under water to drown her. Sometime during this murder, he managed to commit an act of rape. Whether this was before or after death, I have not been able to ascertain.

Mr. Gilmer hid the bodies. Later, a helicopter would be used to search for them. Gilmer, his thirst for rape and assault not yet slaked, kidnapped a young co-worker only a short time later. Driving her to Tippecanoe State Park, he there confined and repeatedly raped her, later unaccountably releasing her alive. Perhaps his inner demons were finally nearly glutted.

The bodies of Jason and Kimberly Tuzinski were found hidden around a mile apart, Kimberly Tuzinski's body being found in a tributary of the Salt Creek River.

Gilmer was picked up for a weapons violation. He plead guilty eventually, avoiding the death penalty, but receiving the grand total of a trio of life sentences without the possibility of parole.

November of 2003, almost exactly *nine years* later, he comitted suicide in his cell. He was being held at a prison facility for the mentally ill. We aren't told, exactly, *how* he took his own life. (I imagine since it was in his prison cell, most likely hanging with a towel or sheet, or with his own belt.)

Very well, then. Out of his three victims, perhaps it was fitting that he himself was his last. (It's a feel-good story all the way around.)

The 1990s, for myself, will always be a deeply troubling time, an anxiety-ridden "calm before the storm," which perched in dread on the cusp of the millennium. Oliver Stone's notorious film Natural Born Killers was released the same year the Tuzinskis were murdered. On the soundtrack, singer Leonard Cohen intones, in his famous, rasping, smoke-choked velvet croon, that he's seen the future, murder . . .

Old men live with long shadows. Voices echo down the corridor of time. Faces swim up from the ocean of memory in the wee hours of the morning when we find sleep impossible. We look at a weathered headstone, beneath which rests the body of a person we once knew, knew when they were young and vibrant and alive. And, somehow, we can't make the connection between the past and what *has passed*; it seems as if we could go through a doorway and be back there, in that long hallway, listening to an idiot kid sing stupid pop songs.

But that was twenty years ago, and the kid is long dead. And time, that cryptic ideogram, has etched deep lines into my face and forehead. And minutes tick by in the vast gloom of my age.

AFTERWORD

The Killing of the King

I am writing this just beyond the fabled Ides of March.

Ceaser, Emporer of Rome, was warned in a prophetic dream to "beware the Ides of March." March 15th, to be exact. He steeled himself against fright, unsuspecting of the conspiracy, led by the treasonous and false Brutus, the doom that was arraigned against him.

It has been over a decade since I have read Julius Ceaser by William Shakespeare. In a story I composed in 2010, a short piece I called "The Tyrant," the "Killing of the King" is described thusly:

"The faces of my troops were set in hard shadows, and, as they circled I saw the glint of cold steel flash forth, and indescribable pain wracked my lungs.I fell forward, spilling a pool of crimson beneath me, and the soldiers leapt upon me to complete the grim task of regicide. Finally, pierced through the body as if I had been shot with a volley of arrows, I faded into blackness as the shadow of death played upon me.

> I was hefted up and out the door, mortally wounded, and hoisted by rope to the walls outside. There I regained consciousness for a flickering few moments, but it was long enough to see a hellish glimpse of the hate-maddened throng to which my carcass was being offered as penance.

> Twisted, curled, blackened faces, deformed by plague, made hollow by hunger, scowled and grimaced and raged below, their black eyes burning pools of pure delirium; accursed filthy faces of a maddened mob whose great thirst for retribution could only be quenched by draining the last drop of blood from out of my wounded form. I had never, in all my wildest fantasies of pain and horror, seen such a spectacle of ugliness as the vile, filthy sea of peasants which surged and undulated and swelled below me. I knew this was the end.
>
> I could still move my arm a bit, and with the last bit of strength I possessed, I reached up to wipe the blood that was dripping from my brow and into my eyes.
>
> Suddenly, and without the slightest warning, the mask—that horrible thing of soft, yielding, fleshly substance which had delivered me to this sorry fate—came away in my bloody palm, revealing for the first time in many years the true face of the man who had so long been possessed by its odious influence and its grim charade.
>
> The false face fell away in my hand, floating feather-like into the swirling sea of shadow below . . ."

I could not have foreseen, five years ago, the country on the cusp of such overwhelming turmoil. Shootings have become endemic, terrorism is rife, the economy is in turmoil, racial strife is becoming inflamed, riots have broken out in Baltimore and Ferguson, Missouri, among other places, and Chicago is one continuous bloodbath, with someone being shot there every fifty-two minutes on one particular day. The people are veering crazily between left wing and right wing demagogues, and the "Killing of the King" does not seem like a ritualized scene out of an ancient play, but a real, alive, vital possibility.

Power wears many masks, many disguises. The late conspiracy writer James Shelby Downard, in his monumental paean to paranoid theorizing King/Kill 33, laid out what he believed to be the ritualized assassination of President John F. Kennedy by a high-ranking contingent of Freemasons, reading even into the very topography of Dealey Plaza the naked face of the conspiracy.

Far be it for me to try and summarize the astounding conclusions of the late Mr. Downard. Suffice it to say, he sees purpose and meaning in the tiniest minutiae of detail, as if the microcosm truly reflected the macrocosm, as if everything was simply another doll in a collection of Russian dolls, each opening up to a smaller and smaller version. As above, so below, those in occult circles might maintain.

Today, crowds of disaffected youth might well call for the "Killing of the King." Is it 1969, 1970, all over again? Maybe much worse, as we drift further and further from our moorings in traditional life. Cast adrift, without a rudder or map to chart the course, and in an environment in which so many factions are pulling in so many different directions, in which people behind an Internet screen become less and less objectively "real"; is it any wonder youth lose their bearings, follow leaders blindly, or simply commit themselves to personal and social destruction?

Jarrod Loughner, James Holmes, Adam Lanza—the names of the killers come too fast, too frequently these days for us to keep up. We hide in our homes, feel happy and contented if we're are simply allowed to go about our business unmolested, to see our little corner of the world through the digitized lens of a social media screen. Truly, the culture is coming apart.

Changes explode across the landscape like blossoming bombs. People are angry, discontented, disconnected.

Robert Oppenheimer said: "I am become Shiva, the destroyer of worlds." This was at Trinity, when he beheld his handiwork—the atom bomb.

Thousands of years before, Heraclitus said: "Fire shall come, and judge and condemn *all* things. Leave rest and quiet to the dead, where they belong . . ."

Both men, separated by the centuries, both beholding in the burning bright rays of the all-consuming, prophetic fire, the final annihilation of man.

Savitri Devi, Hitler's "high priestess," in her culturally proscribed metaphysical meditation on the cyclic nature of time, The Lightning and the Sun, envisioned a world steadily and surely unwinding, deteriorating rapidly, in this Kali-Yuga, this "Age of Gloom."

Soon, religious fanatics might secure for themselves a nuclear device. Our complete destruction is their salvation—or so they believe. Will this herald the Final Battle, the last great conflagration of the human species? Will "Fire come, and judge, and condemn *all* things . . ." as Heraclitus has suggested?

Will a space-faring race comb through the ashes and dust ten thousand million years from now, on the charred remains of a burned-out cinder, a once startlingly blue ovoid sphere lost in the vast firmament of black? Will they find our blackened bones, our temples, citadels, and fast-food restaurants?

Will they read in our cryptic demise the Ideogram of Hate?

Love?

Or, maybe, nothing at all?

Fin.

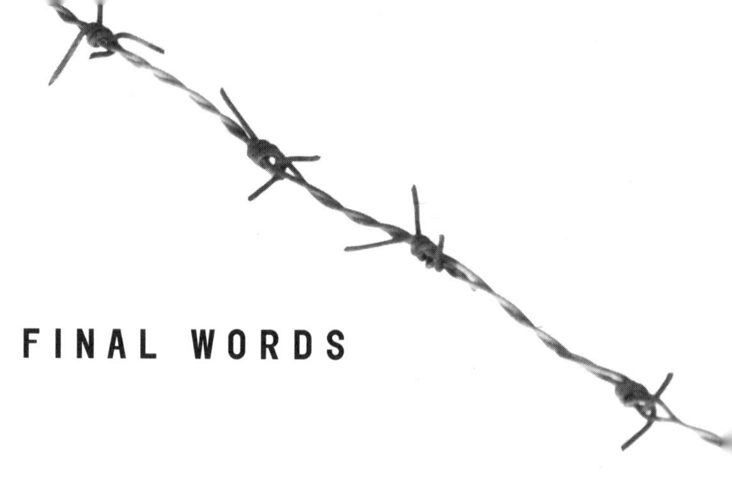

FINAL WORDS

"A Hideous Throng Rush Out."

In the election season of 2016, when American politics seem to be dominated by both Far Right and Far Left demagogues (as exemplified by Donald Trump and Hillary Clinton), the watchword on everyone's lips is "terror." After several religiously spurred bloodbaths, the world is reeling, with some calling for combat, others for "peace."

I wonder: What could these individuals possibly mean?

What is "peace"? Why is it any more desirable than so-called violence, or strife?

Isn't killing and bloodshed the natural state of mankind? As the pseudonymous author Ragnar Redbeard intoned in his scandalous book Might Is Right (1890): "Are we not all predatory animals? If humans ceased wholly from preying upon each other, could they continue to exist?"

I can quote other scandalous wordsmiths. Nietzsche wrote:

> Examine the life of the best and most productive men and nations, and ask yourselves whether a tree which is to grow proudly skywards can dispense with bad weather and storms. Whether misfortune and opposition, or every kind of hatred, jealousy, stubbornness, distrust, severity, greed,

and violence do not belong to the favourable conditions without which a great growth even of virtue is hardly possible?

The Hitlerian Hindu mystic Savitri Devi put it more succinctly in her book, The Lightning and the Sun, when she wrote: "Peace is not the law of action in a fallen world."

Indeed, racial conflict, religious strife, class envy, economic depression, resurgent communism, militarism, racism, nationalism, paranoia, millennial terrors grown fat and fulsome . . . technological marvels and madnesses, the sickening outgrowth of a degenerate age. An Epoch of Homicide . . .

Christ intoned that there would be "wars and rumors of wars . . ."

I might quote Yeats: "Things fall apart, the center does not hold . . . mere anarchy is loosed upon the world . . . Surely, the Second Coming is at hand."

Even better, I might close with a few words from Edgar Allen Poe: "A Hideous throng rush out forever. And laugh— *but smile no more*."

"THIS IS NOT AN EXIT."
—Brett Easton Ellis, American Psycho

APPENDIX A

The Killing of J

He was a guy I first met in a youth psychiatric institution. He was singing Pink Floyd songs in isolation as I walked in. I started singing with him. We soon made friends.

> I spent six months in that place, living with him and two other guys in a dorm room. I was only a kid. When I left, it was understood I would return for checkup visits. I went back one time as an outpatient. The last time I saw him, he gave me a comic book about the Sex Pistols.

I next saw him on the six o'clock news. His picture, and that of his wife, suddenly appeared, with the news that the "mentally impaired" couple had been murdered. I sat there numb. He had written me some letters a couple of years earlier.

I found his grave, years later, searching online. Some memorial website. It was weird looking at an old tombstone for someone you still, subconsciously, very much thought of as young and alive. I also found a newspaper article about the killing. This is based on what happened.

Frank was the next door neighbor in the trailer park. He was a sex offender who had previously done ten years for raping a girl. He must have focused in on my friend and his wife, a young couple, because they were so innocent and naïve. Perhaps he began to want J's wife. (I'll just call him J, okay?) He must have lusted after her, just like he lusted after the young girl he was imprisoned for raping.

He must have pretended to be their friend. Perhaps he made up excuses to come over and borrow stuff. Perhaps he and his wife became nags, a nuisance, but J and his wife were too nice to say anything about it. Perhaps they were secretly afraid.

Or perhaps they suspected nothing at all.

Frank's mind must have been swirling with pornographic images, forbidden lusts, dreams of what he wanted to do, the macabre violence he wanted to enact. Do you imagine he planned the whole thing out, visualized it in his mind, the night before? Did he consciously know he was going to beat and fuck his next door neighbor into oblivion? Did he cogitate on the consequences? Was his animal self even aware?

Frank invited J on a hunting trip. A hunting trip. J decided that he couldn't say no. They went out to a secluded spot, far from the shitty, run-to-riot smell of the trailer park. J suspected nothing. Then, at some point, Frank used a hatchet to beat J's head into a bloody pulp.

Have you ever seen such wounds? I have. I've seen all sorts of homicide photos. The brutality and carnage must have been appalling.

J died easily. His wife would not be so lucky.

Frank went back to the trailer for J's wife. He told her there had been an accident, and J was hurt bad. She panicked, got in the car, went out with him to the woods. There must have been a confused moment when she looked around for her husband, but he was nowhere to be seen. She must have turned to Frank in confusion. Then he exploded. The beast within came out in full rage, and he grabbed J's wife, pushing her to the ground and tearing at her jeans. He raped her brutally, violating her in every way his lust-maddened mind could conceive, before putting his hands around her throat.

He strangled her then. He choked the life out of her as his passion soared skyward, his eyes rolled back in their sockets.

It was ecstasy.

He dumped the bodies in a shallow grave. He was captured and quickly confessed. The bodies were recovered. A funeral was held for two twenty-something kids who had had their whole lives ahead of them. Years later, a picture of J's headstone would be found by ME, on the internet.

Frank went to death row I think. That was eighteen years ago, but he might still be there. I wonder if he relishes, still, what he did in those few hours of rape and murder, or if it seems like the actions of another man, a man who was driven by devils too esoteric to ever fully comprehend. That is, if he hasn't already been executed for his crimes, or died a lonely death.

APPENDIX B

The Tyrant

Last night I dreamt that everyone in the world chose different faces. Each face bore with it an entirely new identity, and as each fleshly mask was applied to one in the now shuffling, blind, faceless, idiot throng, that individual began to assume the characteristics, and then even the life, represented by that face.

I became an emperor. I was master of untold marching legions; I was a lord of great wealth and had at his command bustling, untold numbers of servants and underlings willing to fulfill my every whim. My palace was an architectural wonder the likes of which has never been surpassed by any structure ever erected. The floors were adorned in solid gold, the walls carved delicately from ivory and encrusted with glittering jewels and covered with tapestries of ancient delicate weave and extraordinary design.

These tapestries revealed the history of my noble lineage, and the endless wars and conquests that we could claim as our proud history. Each bloody step of our evolution as a dynasty was displayed, and the bitter vengeance of my antecedents must have made many a subject quiver in terror at the thought of arousing my implacable anger.

Of fleshly pleasures I can swear that there are none I didn't indulge prodigiously; countless triumphal feasts were celebrated, and my table was always heaped with the choicest delicacies and finest, most sumptuous dishes as could be imported from the four corners of my vast kingdom.

Fine wine flowed like rivers of blood down the gullets of my guests; I was a master of ceremonies unparalleled in any era of history. Many were the joys and drunken delights of my fellow feasters, as we made sport of royal clown or jester under the burning torches of my imperial banquet hall. If a particular performer failed to entertain, he could be cast into the dungeon. If he gave offense of any sort, he could be crucified.

Of women I had hundreds, and, indeed, could have had any wench I fancied, as all women anywhere in my kingdom were mine to dispose with as I so desired. Dark, wanton pleasures of the flesh and sensual delights were my chief occupation, and lascivious practices of every stripe were celebrated as I lit the bonfires of brazen passion and made slaves of whatever object tickled my amorous attention. Mad orgies and profane debauches took place in the perfume and incense-wafted abodes and bedchambers of my sinister keep. And, if any wench resisted, or failed to properly satisfy the depraved lusts of my quivering form, she could be burnt alive, beheaded, pulled to pieces on the rack, or crucified.

My generals won many an awesome, bloody conflict under the banner of my merciless reign. My troops stormed into villages and cities, sacked towns, laid siege to castles of dripping stone, and spread like thunder across the face of the earth. Everywhere they spread the mighty fires of my wrath and vengeance, putting whole civilizations to the flame, pillaging and looting and enslaving until the very planet seemed to tremble under my sandaled foot. From these far-flung military adventures they brought back tribute, slaves, many fine and rare spices and treasures, and strange and terrible scrolls of arcane lore.

Of my family I can say but little. Any threat to my power as supreme lord was instantly and cruelly dealt with, whether by poison, or imprisonment, or by some ghastly bit of intrigue planned and plotted expertly and efficiently. I dealt with an insolent cousin by having his tongue removed; I poisoned my firstborn son.

I desired my brother's wife, so had the spineless wretch stationed to a distant military outpost, where the captain of the guard had been well-paid to assure his untimely demise.

Servants I dealt with in a more playful, prankish manner. Once, I conspired to hide some cheap trinket amongst the possessions of a serving girl who had dared rebuff my amorous advances. I hastily called the guard, and upon searching the servant's quarters, they found the object (which, on the whole was of little value).

Immediately she was cast into prison, and then sentenced to hundreds of lashes. She was burned, barely alive, at the stake.

Undoubtedly, I was a god in the world of simpering, ordinary, cowardly men. I knew no fear and wanted for nothing. Filled to bursting with the glory of myself, I at last threw away the religion of my forbears and, seizing the temples, replaced the images of God therein with an image of myself.

At last, I sent out a decree among the peoples of my vast empire that they must now worship me, and that should they fail in doing so, it would mean death for them and their people.

Men reeled in horror at this profane, blasphemous suggestion, and many secret cabals began to mutter among themselves as the growing legions of mendicants strode in slow mobs of despair to the altar of my image.

Undoubtedly, it was one of the last strokes upon the back of the people that they were willing to bear.

Not many months later, a dire famine began to sweep the land, and a pestilence of unknown and horrific origin followed. Men grew hideous with bursting purple sores, and the howling and terror of the night gave way to bonfires of bodies, fed by the heaving wooden carts of corpse collectors who trundled through the village streets at dawn, exclaiming "Bring out your dead! Bring out your dead! Bring out your dead!" all the while ringing a ghastly bell.

The bodies were consigned to the flame, but where kindling was sparse, they were unceremoniously deposited in one of the many yawning pits, with hundreds of others—pits that now dotted the countryside like pocks on a fevered face.

Death by starvation, however, was just as frequent, and my nobles began to grumble that they were starting to fear their own subjects. I paid no mind to such paltry complaints; and indeed, when open rebellion broke out in certain remote provinces, I sent a garrison of troops to crush it beneath an iron heel. The leaders of such rebellions were, with much pomp and circumstance, brought back to the imperial city, paraded as captives through the streets, and left hanging at the gates of the city as a warning against further rebellions.

I pushed my tax collectors mercilessly, commanding them to exact a huge portion of the dwindling wealth of my overburdened, diseased, and now starving subjects. The more the people suffered, the harder I squeezed, until, finally, entire families were starving to death in their homes, and beggars in the street became as numerous as the swarms of flies that followed in their footsteps.

I rebuffed any murmurs of protest from my guards, who began to complain that their forces were stretched thin and that the populace was growing riotous and frenzied with anger. I let all protests against my conduct fall on deaf ears. I continued to enjoy my life of opulent and lavish splendor in the midst of the most dire poverty and want.

Finally, one bloody night, the people of my city, armed with sticks and stones and torches, began to storm the walls of my keep, pushing ladders upward to scale the walls and go over the top. These maniacal revolutionaries were beaten back, sliced to ribbons by soldiers stationed on the walls, or deluged by hot lead poured from boiling cauldrons. My troops sent down black volleys of arrows into the teeming throng, but still they surged forward in defiance. They were hungry for my blood (as well as for food) and more ladders went up, and arrows and stones were shot from the enraged crowd below.

I cowered in my throne room, bellowing, "Kill them! Kill them all! Burn them alive, the traitorous rabble! I'll have every one of their heads hanging from a pike by dawn! Be merciless, and slay the women and children as well! Cut them down where they stand!"

My royal guards gathered around me, dark and troubling looks beetling their brows. My councilors had taken a place in the shadows of the room, and, as my guards circled me, I began to thank them foolishly, saying "Yes! Yes! My loyal troops! You have always served me well, and have I not always returned your loyalty in kind with great payment in riches? Come, let us fly from the mad scene that awaits us outside, through the ancient caverns beneath this castle, and secure me in a safe place of exile until we can regain control of the situation once again!"

The faces of my troops were set in hard shadows, and, as they circled I saw the glint of cold steel flash forth, and indescribable pain wracked my lungs.

I fell forward, spilling a pool of crimson beneath me, and the soldiers leapt upon me to complete the grim task of regicide. Finally, pierced through the body as if I had been shot with a volley of arrows, I faded into blackness as the shadow of death played upon me.

I was hefted up and out the door, mortally wounded, and hoisted by rope to the walls outside. There I regained consciousness for a flickering few moments, but it was long enough to see a hellish glimpse of the hate-maddened throng to which my carcass was being offered as penance.

Twisted, curled, blackened faces, deformed by plague, made hollow by hunger, scowled and grimaced and raged below, their black eyes burning pools of pure delirium, accursed filthy faces of a maddened mob whose great thirst for retribution could only be quenched by draining the last drop of blood from out of my wounded form. I had never, in all my wildest fantasies of pain and horror, seen such a spectacle of ugliness as the vile, filthy sea of peasants which surged and undulated and swelled below me. I knew this was the end.

I could still move my arm a bit, and with the last bit of strength I possessed, I reached up to wipe the blood that was dripping from my brow and into my eyes.

Suddenly, and without the slightest warning, the mask–that horrible thing of soft, yielding, fleshly substance that had delivered me to this sorry fate—came away in my bloody palm, revealing for the first time in many years the true face of the man that had so long been possessed by its odious influence and its grim charade.

The false face fell away in my hand, floating feather-like into the swirling sea of shadow below, and I looked down with the original eyes of one who has awoke from a long and troubled dream.

As they cast me from the top of the wall, into the maelstrom below, and as filthy fingers ripped my flesh to pieces in an insane rampage of utter hate, I knew that I was not responsible for this sorry ending, nor was my punishment just.

For the mob sought to destroy the reign of an evil tyrant, but the tyrant was simply a role played by an idiot, a mere child. And, though they strike down the body, they would never, I knew, destroy that which they so hated. For the mask would find someone else to wear, and the face would change forms, and the mad theatre of horror and revolt would continue forevermore.

Bibliography

Agrawal, Anil. *Necrophilia: Forensic and Medico-Legal Aspects.* Boca Raton, FL: CRC Press, 2011.

Blum, Daniel C. *A Pictorial History of the Silent Screen.* New York: Grossett and Dunlap, 1972.

Brown, Kelly R. *Florence Lawrence, The Biograph Girl: America's First Movie Star.* Jefferson, NC: McFarland and Co., 1999.

Burrough, Bryan. *Public Enemies: America's Greatest Crime Wave and the Birth of the FBI, 1933–1934.* New York: Penguin, 2004.

Cosel, Carl von. *The Lost Diary of Count von Cosel.* Key West, FL: Phantom Press, 2011.

Devi, Savitri. *The Lightning and the Sun.* Hillsboro, WV: National Vanguard Books, 2000.

Downward, James Shelby. "King/Kill 33." *Apocalypse Culture*, Ed. Adam Parfrey, 1st Edition, Amok Press, Los Angeles, 1987.

Ellis, Brett Easton. *American Psycho.* New York: Vintage, 1991.

Ellsworth, Monte. *The Bath School Disaster (1927)*, (Web) http://daggy.name/tbsd/tbsd-x.html.

Finbow, Steve. *Grave Desire: A Cultural History of Necrophilia.* Zero Books, 2014.

Fussell, Betty Harper. *Mabel: America's First "I-Don't-Care" Girl.* New Haven, CT: Ticknor and Fields, 1982.

Greene, Robert. *The 48 Laws of Power.* New York: Penguin, 2000.

Haining, Peter. *Cannibal Killers: Murderers Who Kill and Eat Their Victims.* London: Constable, 2008.

Harrison, Ben. *Undying Love: The True Story of a Passion That Defied Death.* Key West, FL: Ketch and Yawl Press, 2009.

Jones, Aphrodite. *All She Wanted.* New York: Gallery Books, 2008.

Martin, Christopher Hawley. *Urges: A Chronicle of Serial Killer Larry Hall.* North Charleston, SC: CreateSpace Independent Publishing Platform, 2010.

Morton, Jim. "Karen Greenlee: The Unrepentant Necrophile." *Apocalypse Culture*, Ed. Adam Parfrey, Amok Press, Los Angeles, CA, 1989.

Nash, Jay Robert. *Bloodletters and Badmen.* Lanham, MD: M. Evans & Company, 1995.

Nietzsche, Friedrich. *Beyond Good and Evil: Prelude to a Philosophy of the Future.* Marion, IN: Zem Books, 2016.

Poe, Edgar Allen. *Complete Tales and Poems.* New York: Castle Books, 2002.

Ramsland, Katherine. "John Norman Collins, The Co-Ed Killer." Murderpedia (Web) www.murderpedia.org/male.C/c/collins-john-norman.htm.

Redbeard, Ragnar. *Might Is Right.* Marion, IN: Zem Books, 2015.

Schechter, Harold. *Deviant: The Shocking True Story of Ed Gein, the Original Psycho.* New York: Gallery Books, 1998.

Toland, John. *The Dillinger Days.* Boston: Capo Press, 1998.

Woods, Paul Anthony. *Ed Gein—Psycho!* New York: St. Martin's Griffin, 1995.